Placements and Work-based Education Studies

Written specifically for education studies students, this accessible text offers a clear introduction to placements and work-based learning, providing an insight into work in schools and education settings.

Including case studies to illustrate the diversity of placements and workplace opportunities, it explores the theory and practice of working in educational contexts and supports students as they develop the skills and aptitudes that enhance their employability. With the aim of helping students to prepare for and get the most out of their work placements, chapters include:

- the nature of work-based learning on placement;

- preparing for your placement;

- placements in schools and other educational settings;

- learning on field trips and study visits;

- working with students with specific learning difficulties/dyslexia on placement;

- international placements.

Part of the *Foundations of Education Studies* series, this textbook is essential reading for students undertaking courses in Childhood Studies, Child and Youth Studies and Education Studies.

Jim Hordern is Senior Lecturer in Education Studies at Bath Spa University, UK.

Catherine A. Simon is Programme Leader in Education Studies and Award Leader for the Education Specialised Award at Bath Spa University, UK.

Foundations of Education Studies Series

This is a series of books written specifically to support undergraduate education studies students. Each book provides a broad overview to a fundamental area of study exploring the key themes and ideas to show how these relate to education. Accessibly written with chapter objectives, individual and group tasks, case studies and suggestions for further reading, the books will give students an essential understanding of the key disciplines in education studies, forming the foundations for future study.

Philosophy and Education: An introduction to key questions and themes
Joanna Haynes, Ken Gale and Mel Parker

Research and Education
Will Curtis, Mark Murphy and Sam Shields

Policy and Education
Paul Adams

Psychology and Education
Diahann Gallard and Katherine M. Cartmell

Placements and Work-based Learning in Education Studies: An introduction for students
Edited by Jim Hordern and Catherine A. Simon

Forthcoming titles

Sociology and Education
Richard Waller and Chrissie Rogers

Placements and Work-based Learning in Education Studies

An introduction for students

Edited by Jim Hordern
and Catherine A. Simon

Routledge
Taylor & Francis Group

LONDON AND NEW YORK

First published 2017
by Routledge
2 Park Square, Milton Park, Abingdon, Oxon OX14 4RN

and by Routledge
711 Third Avenue, New York, NY 10017

Routledge is an imprint of the Taylor & Francis Group, an informa business

British Library Cataloguing in Publication Data
A catalogue record for this book is available from the British Library

Library of Congress Cataloging in Publication Data
A catalog record for this book has been requested

ISBN: 978-1-138-83906-9 (hbk)
ISBN: 978-1-138-83907-6 (pbk)
ISBN: 978-1-315-73364-7 (ebk)

Typeset in Bembo
by Wearset Ltd, Boldon, Tyne and Wear

Contents

Contributors

Editors

Jim Hordern is Senior Lecturer in Education Studies at Bath Spa University, UK.

Catherine A. Simon is Programme Leader in Education Studies at Bath Spa University, UK.

Contributors

June Bianchi is Senior Lecturer in Arts Education at Bath Spa University, UK.

Joe Brown is Programme Leader in Early Years Initial Teacher Training at Bath Spa University, UK.

Dan Davies is Dean of the Cardiff School of Education at Cardiff Metropolitan University, UK.

Mary Dooley is Senior Lecturer in Education Studies at Bath Spa University, UK.

Martine Duggan is Programme Leader in Primary and Early Years PGCE at Bath Spa University, UK.

Laura Green is Senior Lecturer in Education Studies (Sociology) at Bath Spa University, UK.

Lone Hattingh is Senior Lecturer and Award Leader for MA Education, Early Years at Bath Spa University, UK.

Richard Riddell is Senior Lecturer in Education Studies at Bath Spa University, UK.

Nick Sorensen is Associate Dean at Bath Spa University, UK.

Abbreviations

ADHD	Attention Deficit Hyperactivity Disorder
AHRC	Arts and Humanities Research Council
AIDS	Acquired Immune Deficiency Syndrome
ASBO	Anti-Social Behaviour Order
ASDAN	Award Scheme Development and Accreditation Network
BA	Bachelor of Arts
BDA	British Dyslexia Association
BEd	Bachelor of Education
BERA	British Education Research Association
BME	Black and Minority Ethnic
BPS	British Psychological Society
BSc	Bachelor of Science
CV	Curriculum Vitae
DBS	Disclosure and Barring Service
DCMS	Department for Culture, Media and Sport
DfE	Department for Education
ELT	Experiential Learning Theory
EU	European Union
EYE	Early Years Educator
EYFS	Early Years Foundation Stage
EYSEFD	Early Years Sector-Endorsed Foundation Degree
EYTS	Early Years Teacher Status
FE	Further Education
GCSE	General Certificate of Secondary Education
GDP	Gross Domestic Product
HE	Higher Education

ICT	Information and Communication Technology
INSET	In-Service Training Day
ITE	Information Technology Equipment
ITT	Initial Teacher Training
IWB	Inter-Active Whiteboard
LAC	Looked After Children
MFMC	My Future My Choice
NEET	Not in Education, Employment or Training
NGOs	Non-Governmental Organisations
NS-SEC	National Statistics Socio-Economic Classification
NUT	National Union of Teachers
NYA	National Youth Agency
Ofsted	Office for Standards in Education, Children's Services and Skills
PATOSS	Professional Association for Teachers and Assessors of Students with Specific Learning Difficulties
PGCE	Post Graduate Certificate in Education
PMP	Professional Master's Programme
QAA	Quality Assurance Agency
QTS	Qualified Teacher Status
SEN	Special Educational Needs
SENCO	Special Educational Needs Co-Ordinator
SEND	Special Educational Needs and Disability
SpLD	Specific Learning Difficulty
STEM	Science, Technology, Engineering and Mathematics
TA	Teaching Assistant
UCAS	University and Colleges Admissions Service
UK	United Kingdom
UN	United Nations
UNCRC	United Nations Convention on the Rights of the Child
WBL	Work-Based Learning

Placement and work-based learning in education studies

Introduction

Section A

Jim Hordern

Placements and work-based learning are key elements of many undergraduate programmes in education studies. Gaining experience of workplace contexts is widely considered to be vitally important for students of education. This is partly because the study of education is closely connected in many institutions with the professional preparation of teachers and other professionals working in educational contexts. However it is also because experiences of educational practice are seen as important for critically engaging with educational theory and with some of the key debates about the role of education in society. This book provides a thorough overview of the nature of placement and work-based learning in education studies, with a primary focus on the context of education studies undergraduate programmes in the United Kingdom. Despite the predominance of examples and arguments that relate to the United Kingdom, much of what is discussed here may also have application to experiences of students in other countries. The first part of the book (Section A) concentrates on providing a general and conceptual introduction, concentrating on the rationale for placements and work-based learning, the contexts in which placement and work-based experiences occur, the nature of work-based learning, preparing for placements and the role of work-based assessment. In the second part of the book (Section B) placements and work-based learning are examined in different contexts, which include schools, cultural settings, early years settings and youth and community work. Different issues and dimensions are also explored in this second part, including working with students with learning difficulties on placement, international aspects of placements and the significance of field trips and study visits.

All the chapters in this book aim to help students engage with the nature of placement and work-based learning through suggested activities, which may involve investigation, reflection or analysis. The authors have also signposted key further reading for deeper understanding of the topics discussed, enabling students to extend their knowledge and awareness in those areas that are of particular interest. Students using this book may wish to start with Section A to gain awareness of general issues that relate to placement and work-based learning in education studies, or jump immediately to those chapters in Section B that particularly relate to the placement and work-based experiences that they have had or are preparing to experience. The book is therefore structured to meet the needs of individual students who may choose to return to it to consult different chapters as they progress through the course.

The first two chapters of Section A are intended to provide a general introduction to the topic, mapping out some of the terrain. In Chapter 1 Jim Hordern presents an overview of placement and work-based learning in education studies, starting with a discussion of the emergence of education studies degrees in England over time and their relationship to forms of teacher education and other academic disciplines. He examines the rationale for placement and work-based learning in education studies and identifies what placements and work-based learning can offer students. In Chapter 2 Hordern focuses on the context of placements and work-based learning, locating workplaces within broader organisational, social, political and economic contexts. He investigates the extent to which workplace processes and activities provide access to specific knowledge and competence, and to distinctive forms of learning. This then moves into a discussion of what students can learn from their experience of workplace activities while on an education studies programme.

In Chapter 3 Nick Sorensen provides a theoretical discussion of the nature of work-based learning that occurs on placement. He examines why learning in the workplace is important, what it entails and how that learning occurs. He discusses why reflective practice needs to be seen as an important feature of continuing professional development (CPD) with reference to a masters level programme, and connects this to the experiences of undergraduates on education studies degrees. In Chapter 4 Catherine Simon focuses on issues around preparing for placements including how to choose a placement that is right for you and how to negotiate university, placement and personal expectations. She also discusses some of the risks connected with placements, discussing what to do when things go wrong and the practicalities of insurance, health and safety and safeguarding. These are all especially important when undertaking placements and work-based activities in educational settings. She also covers the role of a reflective journal in establishing a structured way to organising your learning on placement. In Chapter 5 Joe Brown discusses the nature of work-based assessment and how it is typically assessed on university-level programmes. He explores the different types of knowledge, skills and professional capabilities which work-based assessment aims to develop and how students can recognise these in the assignments they are undertaking. He highlights the importance of critical reflection and collaboration, and outlines some reflective activities and example assignments. He also tackles the ethical requirements of work-based assessment.

We hope you enjoy this book and find its contents useful as a starting point for thinking about the nature of placements and work-based learning in education studies. Please feel free to get in touch with the authors if you have any comments or feedback!

1

Overview of placement and work-based learning in education studies

Jim Hordern

Purpose of the chapter

After reading this chapter you should understand:

- the origins of education studies degrees and how placement and work-based learning contributes;
- why placement and work-based learning is important in education studies;
- what placement and work-based learning can offer you.

Introduction

1 How have education studies degrees developed and what can placement and work-based learning contribute?

Education studies undergraduate degrees have increased in number considerably in recent times in England as a response to changes both in teacher education policy and in the structure of higher education (Burton and Bartlett 2006; Furlong 2013; Ward 2008). The majority of these are classified as 'academic studies in education' and do not lead to qualified teacher status in themselves. The academic study of education was once seen as an important component of teacher education in England, with the 'foundation disciplines' of philosophy, sociology, history and psychology of education strongly influencing the curriculum of the growing numbers of undergraduate Bachelor of Education (BEd) degrees in the 1970s taken by many seeking to qualify as a primary school teacher (Furlong 2013). However when these foundation disciplines were brought together with more 'practical' teaching preparation elements in the courses, the consequence was sometimes an 'unhappy relationship' (Ward 2008: 17), with programmes that lacked coherence. Teacher education at that time was largely offered by local authority controlled colleges of education (offering undergraduate courses), and there were also some postgraduate courses offered by universities. As has been documented in detail by Furlong (2013) and Burton and Bartlett (2006), policy changes from the 1980s onwards in respect of teacher education undermined the undergraduate BEd degrees and increased postgraduate provision, with the Postgraduate Certificate in Education (PGCE) eventually becoming the mainstream entry route into teaching in both primary and secondary education in England. While teacher educators had at one time had considerable control over the curriculum, by the 1990s power was firmly in the hands of a government agency (the Teacher Training Agency established in 1994), which was responsible for specifying what teacher education programmes should contain. The consequence of this was that teacher education programmes moved away from an 'educational' disciplinary base and concentrated to a greater extent on school experience, professional studies and enhancing subject knowledge (Furlong 2013; Whitty 2014). Workplace experience became increasingly valued, a development that many applauded. However, this may have come at the expense of providing new teachers with the academic resources to make sense of what they were experiencing in those workplaces, and to distinguish between good and poor teaching practice.

Meanwhile in the 1970s, 1980s and early 1990s, many of the colleges of education became absorbed into the wider higher education system as local authority controlled higher education was dismantled, becoming part of increasingly powerful polytechnics, or the older universities or independent higher education institutions in their own right (Brown 2011). The upshot was that there was greater potential for developing new types of undergraduate degrees in education with curricula controlled again by academic members of staff. Degrees that would be categorised as 'academic studies in education' began to emerge, some which echoed the content and structure of the former BEd degrees previously offered by the colleges (Furlong 2013). One key difference, however, was that these new 'academic' degrees did not lead directly to qualified teacher status, as this would mean conforming to a particular set of government standards or be subject to inspection. Some universities also persisted with undergraduate level teacher education via a bachelor degree, but these courses are in the minority at present in England, while in Scotland a number of universities offer a four-year masters degree which leads to a teaching qualification. Nevertheless, despite the disciplinary or 'academic' focus of many of the education studies programmes, there remains a strong sense that experience in the workplace is important for students of education.

A search of the University and Colleges Admissions Service (UCAS) database during September 2015 revealed that there are over 150 universities and colleges in the United Kingdom offering some form of education-related undergraduate programme. The institutions involved range from some of the oldest and largest institutions in the UK (i.e. Cambridge, Durham, Edinburgh, Glasgow) to a wide range of smaller university centres and colleges (i.e. at Peterborough, Gower, Barnsley or Bury), reflecting considerable demand for the programmes in all parts of the country. The programmes include foundation degrees, one-year top-ups and three-year bachelors programmes. There is enormous diversity, with courses focusing on the early years or early childhood studies, primary education, international education and youth studies, in addition to multiple combinations of joint degrees with other subjects. Education studies can be 'seen as a "subject" defined by its curriculum content and drawing selectively upon ... psychology, sociology, philosophy, history and economics' and can be seen 'as a "discipline" with its own academic community, its own distinctive discourse and methods of enquiry' (QAA 2015: 6). It can also be seen as strongly professionally orientated, providing the 'knowledge, understanding and critical analysis to inform current and future professionals' (QAA 2015: 6).

Placement and work-based learning have an important role in education studies degrees. The subject benchmark statement that sets out the structure of education studies identifies 'learning in the workplace' (QAA 2015: 6) as important for professional development. However, placement and work-based learning also has a broader role – it provides insight into the contexts in which educational processes occur – including 'educational settings, such as administration, post-16 learning, children's services, community development' (QAA 2015: 7). Thus placements and workplace learning can raise awareness of what is common and what differs about education in different contexts, and help develop critical engagement with how policies are put into practice. They are also important sources of material for research projects and investigations, as students have the opportunity to make contacts within institutions and settings and to collect data, providing this is agreed between the host setting and their home institution. It is important, however, to distinguish between the professional development opportunities available at work and the research opportunities. If we want to collect data in workplace settings we must gain the consent of participants, which may include our colleagues, and also managers and supervisors so they are clear what we are trying to achieve and how this might affect work activities.

Analysis of available programme documentation of current undergraduate programmes in education studies at higher education institutions across the South West region of the UK demonstrates the core role of placements and work-based study. All programmes at the six institutions investigated offer placements or work-based learning modules including in schools, early years settings and various voluntary organisations. In some cases placements or work-based learning experiences are compulsory, in others they are optional. Visits to educational settings also feature in some course descriptions, and in all cases the importance of experience of educational practice is emphasised. A brief summary of the findings of this analysis is provided below in Table 1.1:

ACTIVITY 1

- Find the programme handbook for your course. How is your programme described? Is there any discussion of the purpose of the programme? Does this relate to your experience of the programme?

- What is said about placement and work-based learning in the programme handbook? How important are these for the overall programme?

- Do you think an education studies degree should qualify you to become a teacher? Why/ why not?

TABLE 1.1 Institutions offering placement and work-based learning opportunities in South West England

Institution	Placement and work-based learning opportunities
Former college of higher education	Placements are an integral part of the undergraduate degree, and compulsory in the second year. There are work-based routes into the third year of the undergraduate degree via partner colleges. Visits to educational settings and placements characterise many of the modules.
Pre-92 university	One-year placements are available and optional for all undergraduates.
Former polytechnic	Offers an undergraduate degree specifically for those in work in educational settings. Placements are a core element to all education degrees, with a mandatory minimum number of days on placement.
Former polytechnic	Work-based and independent learning opportunities are explicitly linked to professional development and employability.
Former college of higher education	Approximately 50 days of work placement are a core part of the undergraduate degree, and volunteering is strongly encouraged.
Former college of higher education	Opportunities to work in educational settings and to gain workplace experience. This is linked to further study and employment routes.

2 Why is placement and work-based learning important in education studies?

Periods of time in the workplace are thus considered valuable for those undertaking education studies degrees. There are many reasons for this. First, education studies can be described as a 'professionally-orientated' or perhaps a 'practice-orientated' discipline or field that requires some form of first-hand 'acquaintance' (Winch 2010) with educational processes in educational contexts to develop a deep understanding of the nature of education itself (Hordern 2015). Some might argue, however, that this professional or practice orientation is not in keeping with the description of many education studies degrees as 'academic studies in education'. While there can be some tension between the 'academic' and the 'professional', it is important to observe that there are other well-established professional disciplines such as medicine, engineering or architecture that could also be considered fully academic. While the study of education is perhaps more contested than these other professional disciplines, there is no real reason to suggest that the 'professional' and 'academic' cannot be reconciled within an education studies degree. Thus, better understanding the 'practice' of education through workplace experience (which may include research as much as gaining new knowledge and skills) seems to be an important component within such a degree.

Second, a high percentage of students on education studies degrees are likely to be interested in employment in educational institutions and settings. Therefore, including work-based experience within the degree is helpful to give students a better understanding of educational processes and contexts. It is very difficult to get a place on a teacher education programme without experience in a school or early years setting – placements and work-based experiences provide applicants for these programmes with important insights. On placement you are gaining awareness of multiple aspects of how workplaces operate, including:

- how different teachers and practitioners work with children;
- supporting children in their learning;
- workplaces routines, practices and cultures;
- expectations of workplace behaviour;
- interaction with colleagues and parents;
- team-working;
- leadership and management;
- professional judgement;
- managing challenging tasks.

Experience of these different aspects of workplaces is vitally important for students of education studies to gain a better sense of the *practice* of education. By a 'practice' we mean here something like a 'coherent and complex form of socially established cooperative human activity' (MacIntyre 2007: 187), or 'configurations of actions that carry a specific meaning' (Nicolini 2012: 10). In other words educational practice can be understood as *purposeful human activity*. Arguably, different forms of educational practice in very different institutions and settings nevertheless have some common ground. Teaching and supporting children's learning is essentially an activity that is dependent on strong and supportive personal relations and sensitivity to the needs of individual children, young people and adults. It also requires efficient organisation and the capacity for fair and accurate judgement. But, educational practice is broader than classroom teaching and the education and care of young children. It also involves activities such as the organisation and administration of institutions and settings, the development of curricula and production of materials. Educational practice takes place in multiple contexts and is informed or shaped by different traditions, customs and policies. Your placement or work-based learning experience may provide you with access to various settings and enable you to appreciate the diversity of educational practices as you experience different teaching styles and aspects of school or setting life. If you have the opportunity to visit a different institution or setting you are likely to find aspects of educational practice that are similar to your previous experiences and some that are different. This may help you to evaluate which forms of education are particularly beneficial to children and young people and to better understand some of the different theoretical assumptions that underpin these practices.

ACTIVITY 2

- What is important about a placement (or work-based learning) for you? How do you think it contributes to your programme?

- Ask other students what is valuable for them about placements and work-based learning – are their views similar to yours?

- What diverse educational practice have you experienced on placement?

---

3 What placement and work-based learning can offer you

There are considerable advantages to undertaking a placement and learning at work as part of your education studies programme. You are enhancing your employability by becoming familiar with, and involved in, education processes and activities. As noted above, programme leaders for teacher education courses and employers require you to have some experience of the workplace, so your placement or work-based experience offers much. You need to think through how your placement and work-based learning experience complements and builds on your previous experiences and knowledge. You also need to think through how your placement or work-based learning experience is contributing to your professional and per-sonal development. Are you aware of the capabilities that you can develop on your placement?

Placement and work-based learning can be seen as part of a broader path of professional development or 'professional formation', the development of your professional identity, expertise and values. While in work you are learning how to be a professional practitioner – observing and perhaps taking on the behaviours and practices of other professionals in the workplace. This may be the first time you have seen at first-hand how professionals manage the problems of work, and this in itself may be a highly significant learning process. You may appreciate how more experienced professionals make judgements and take action at work, often under pressure of time constraints and while needing to take account of regulations and guidance. You may come across colleagues with a wide variety of different views about their work, education and current policy. You may also experience different styles of leadership, management and supervision, and different ways of organising work and the workplace. All of these may influence your understanding of professional practice and the development of your identity. You can also develop your sense of professional value, and relate the values you experience to your own sense of what is valuable.

You have an excellent opportunity at work to reflect on all forms of educational practices – how teaching is organised, how learning takes place, how curriculum is developed and how policy is implemented. You may take part in school or setting meetings, engage in decision-making with colleagues and contribute to administration and preparation. You may engage in work with parents and other visitors to the school. You should try to relate these experiences to alternative ways in which these things can be done – either that you have experienced in other workplaces or that you have read about in academic or practitioner literature. This should help you to critically reflect on educational processes at work and to think through ways in which they can be improved and how you can justify these improvements.

ACTIVITY 3

■ Make a list of the different types of educational setting that it would be useful for you to experience for your academic and career interests. Which ones have you experienced so far as a pupil, student or employee?

■ Reflect on what you would like to achieve during your placement or work-based experience. How will you ensure you have achieved these objectives? How will you build on these to further your professional development?

Conclusion

Placements and work-based learning are core elements of education studies degrees and are strongly integrated with other elements of these programmes. This is partly due to the historical development of education studies as a professionally-orientated discipline or field, and also to concerns about employability and preparation for further study. The placement or work-based experience that is part of your degree offers opportunities to examine a range of educational practices and to enhance your employability. You may also have opportunities to examine how aspects of educational theory and policy are translated into educational practice. It is important that you make the most of these opportunities.

Follow-up activity

■ Conduct some desk-based research into differing types of placement and work-based experience on offer in your education studies degrees and those at other institutions in your city or regional area. How do these differ? What improvements could you recommend to ensure that students derive more benefits from these experiences?

Further reading

Furlong, J. (2013) *Education: an Anatomy of the Discipline. Rescuing the University Project*. London: Routledge.

Ward, S. (2008) 'Education Studies and Teacher Education'. *Educational Futures* 1 (1): 17–33. http://educationstudies.org.uk/wp-content/uploads/2013/11/ward2.pdf. The British Education Studies

Association website contains some background information on education studies programmes. Its website: http://educationstudies.org.uk/.

References

Burton, D. and Bartlett, S. (2006) 'The Evolution of Education Studies in Higher Education in England'. *The Curriculum Journal* 17 (4): 383–396.

Brown, R. (2011) 'Looking Back, Looking Forward: the Changing Structure of UK Higher Education, 1980–2012'. In Brennan, J. and Shah, T. eds *Higher Education and Society in Changing Times: Looking Back and Looking Forward*. Milton Keynes: CHERI.

Furlong, J. (2013) *Education: an Anatomy of the Discipline. Rescuing the University Project*. London: Routledge.

Hordern, J. (2015) 'Bernstein's Sociology of Knowledge and Education(al) Studies', paper presented at Seminar on Educational Studies – the University Project in Different Jurisdictions, Green Templeton College, University of Oxford, 16 July.

MacIntyre, A. (2007) *After Virtue*. 3rd edn. Notre Dame, Indiana: University of Notre Dame Press.

Nicolini, D. (2012) *Practice Theory, Work & Organisation: an Introduction*. Oxford: OUP.

Quality Assurance Agency (QAA) (2015) Subject Benchmark Statement: Education Studies. Gloucester: QAA.

Whitty, G. (2014) 'Recent Developments in Teacher Training and Their Consequences for the "University Project" in Education'. *Oxford Review of Education* 40 (4): 466–481.

Winch, C. (2010) *Dimensions of Expertise: A Conceptual Exploration of Vocational Knowledge*. London: Continuum.

2

The context of placement and work-based learning

Jim Hordern

Purpose of the chapter

After reading this chapter you should understand:

- how and why workplaces differ;
- what these differences could mean for what and how you can learn;
- some introductory concepts for analysing workplaces learning opportunities.

Introduction

Whether you are going on placement or already in work, you will find that the workplaces you work within will have a significant impact on how and what you learn. Learning within workplaces is shaped by a wide variety of factors, some of which are related to the organisation of which that workplace is a part and the work activities that organisation is concerned with. Other factors may include the interpersonal relations between colleagues and how work is managed within the workplace. What and how you learn within that workplace is also strongly related to your particular disposition to learning – what are you trying to get out of the experience? What action can you take to maximise your learning opportunities? In this chapter we explore some of these ideas and questions in order to support you in better understanding the nature of workplace learning. You will be provided with some conceptual tools that will help you think about your workplace experience and are encouraged to think critically about how that workplace operates and how it can be improved to support your ongoing professional development, and that of your colleagues/co-workers. Some illustrations are offered, primarily from English contexts.

1 The context of learning at work: an overview

Work is generally considered to be purposeful activity, and yet the workplace is not simply a place where workers mechanically undertake tasks and fulfil obligations to meet particular objectives. Work can be social and highly political, with interpersonal relations, friendships and tensions adding a particular flavour to each workplace context. Colleagues may be members of well-functioning teams, or relatively isolated individuals focused on their own specific tasks with little interest in what the person in the next room is doing. There may be clear notions of leadership and obvious individual leaders, or a distinct lack of collective direction. A particular workplace may be quite independent of any other workplace, or it may be part of a wider organisation of workplaces, which may be similar to or different from each other. More broadly, workplaces sit within particular legal, political, economic and societal contexts that shape what is considered to be acceptable and unacceptable activity at work. Employment conditions, management expectations, workplace rituals and routines may differ across organisations and societies (Rainbird et al. 2004). Equally, technological change may result in new workplace practices emerging, and require new ways of learning.

We may encounter a wide variety of workplaces in the study of education, from schools, colleges, early years settings and voluntary sector providers. Each will have its own character, shaped in part by the culture of the organisation of which it is a part. Handy (1993) usefully identifies how organisations can be 'power', 'role', 'task' and 'person' cultures, which define their purpose and operations. A power culture emerges around strong leaders or 'one man bands', who have considerable control over operations of the organisation – this can often be found in small entrepreneurial organisations or pressure groups with charismatic leaders. Role cultures, on the other hand, are bureaucratic with defined rules and procedures, which govern organisational life. They are often stable and resilient, but slow moving and resistant to change. Task cultures are usually problem-focused, often found in organisations developed for a particular project or to achieve a particular goal. Last, person cultures exist when organisations are developed to serve groups of individuals with common interests, often skilled professionals who do not wish to be bound by rules or strong individual leadership. While we might think of schools as more role orientated, there may also be power cultures at work in some small voluntary and private sector organisations, and strong beliefs in a person culture may also be important in some forms of higher education. However, any organisation is likely to be a mix of differing cultures, often in tension with each other and shaped by the wider environment of which they are a part.

Felstead et al. (2009) and Eraut and Hirsch (2007) identify how the broader systems in which workplaces are located influence the extent to which workers have discretion and control over their workplace tasks, factors which are particularly important for learning, and this may differ where certain cultures are prevalent. Where workers have greater discretion and control over their work, they can adapt tasks and processes creatively, innovating and developing new forms of expertise. If workers have limited control and follow a closely prescribed and monitored set of instructions (for example in what or how to teach) then innovation is taken out of their hands and they have less incentive to be independently innovative and creative – they are less likely to feel they own their own work. The nature of management is crucial here in supporting learning. In certain organisational cultures, managers and leaders may be better at 'facilitating' workplace learning, while others may seek to 'control' and specify what is learnt, and how this happens (Eraut and Hirsch 2007; Felstead *et al.* 2009).

School organisations are often thought of as bureaucratic, but may also be driven by inspirational leaders or networks. Schooling reform in England recently has resulted in many local schools becoming academies, sometimes as part of larger independent organisations, often led by high-profile sponsors. Academy schools have governance and management structures which remove the obligation to co-operate with other schools in the local authority area. The managers and headteachers in academy schools have considerable flexibility in the organisation of their workplaces, the terms and conditions of their teaching staff, and in how pupils are taught (NUT 2012). This contrasts with local authority, community or comprehensive schools, where working conditions and processes have often been agreed at a local authority level or as part of a broader agreement. Arguably, the flexibility on offer in an academy could result in teaching staff having considerable discretion and control over their work, but the opposite may also be the case if the management of a particular academy chain or a headteacher decides to prescribe a particular way of working or 'educational formula' that must be followed by all within the school. The 'audit culture' promoted by school inspection regimes may also reduce the scope for teachers to work in the ways that they might wish. The ability of teachers to improve the quality of pedagogy and classroom interaction has been identified as vital for improvements in educational outcomes (Husbands 2013), but this may be compromised if teachers have limited control over their work.

Early years settings are usually considerably smaller than schools, and workplaces can often seem less routinised and work less structured. This could offer early years workers greater control over their work and opportunity to put new ideas into practice. In England, however, curriculum reforms and the ongoing challenges of inspection may constrain practitioner autonomy. Early years provision is fragmented in England, with greater private and voluntary sector provision than is the norm in many other European countries (Penn 2014). This diversity of provision may encourage a greater range of practice within early years workplaces, so that particular settings can pursue their own vision of good quality early years education and care. On the other hand, it may also result in some poor quality practice emerging locally, and in forms of management that are not supportive of the professional development of practitioners (Hordern 2013). The potential for government policy and statutory frameworks to shape workplace culture is matched by the scope for pioneering private individuals to develop their own early years provision and shape workplace practices in ways that they think are important. Indeed, it could be argued that pioneering individuals have been particularly powerful in influencing early years educational traditions (Nutbrown and Clough 2014).

You may also be working or undertaking your placement in a voluntary or community based organisation, and here the diversity of workplace context may be considerable. Some workplaces have very clear roles and responsibilities set out in job descriptions and organisational charts, while others operate a more fluid approach where employees and volunteers may be generally expected to contribute to each and any activity, depending on their capabilities and availability. Arguably, there is greater scope for fast-moving radical change in workplace culture in less bureaucratic organisations, and this may lead to greater uncertainty about the future.

ACTIVITY 1

■   Does the organisation you are working in have clear roles and responsibilities for its employees? Can you find job descriptions and an organisational chart? What do these tell you about the culture of the organisation and what it expects of its employees?

■   How is professional development supported in your place of work? Is there a professional development policy? To what extent do workers have discretion and control over their own professional practice and development?

■   Have your colleagues worked in many different educational organisations? How have the workplace cultures differed?

---

2 The importance of participation

Billett highlights the importance of 'participatory practices', which can be described as involving both 'close personal interactions' and 'engagement in the physical and social environment that constitutes the workplace' (2004: 113). This is learning as participation, recognising the insights of the community of practice tradition (Lave and Wenger 1991) and the importance of the 'social world' for 'knowledge construction' (Billett 2004: 112–113) as emphasised by Vygotskian theorists. Certain forms of participation are particularly beneficial for workers depending on their level of expertise. Thus 'opportunities to observe' or 'secure direct guidance through … interactions between experts and novices' may help to make 'concepts and practices accessible' (ibid.: 114). These opportunities and interactions may be consciously shaped into a 'workplace curriculum' involving 'pathways of activities that are often inherently pedagogical' (ibid.: 119). This can serve the purpose of supporting novice practitioners gain workplace expertise that builds on education they have received in institutions, and may also make use of the experiences they have gained in other workplaces. Some managers and senior leaders in schools and early years settings may structure the workplace activities of novice practitioners so that they can engage in a workplace curriculum, inducting them into workplace practices through participative opportunities and interaction with experts.

However, organisational constraints and workplace pressures may undermine best efforts to offer learning opportunities, either pushing new practitioners into taking on responsibilities too early or restricting their participation if there is limited time to support them gain expertise.

It is important to recognise that we may or may not be aware of how or what we are learning. In other words there can be both 'explicit' and 'tacit' dimensions to learning, knowledge and expertise (Eraut and Hirsch 2007; Winch 2010). The culture of an organisation and the mode of practice we are engaged in may lead us to work in particular ways. We may thus 'tacitly' (without necessarily realising it) take on behaviours, attitudes and techniques that are part of the practice we are engaged in. Those practitioners who have only worked in one educational setting or institution may thus assume that the practice common in their setting or institution is shared more widely than it is. If they take on a role in a setting or institution where very different workplace practices are common it may take them some time to adjust. Workplace learning can also be more 'explicit', with opportunities for colleagues to learn from others through collaborative tasks, problem-solving and mentoring and coaching (Eraut and Hirsch 2007: 25–27). In such situations managers, supervisors and practitioners may identify the learning purpose of the activity and seek to document what has been learnt over time.

For those readers on placement, it is also worth considering the extent to which your temporary stay in the workplace offers you some advantages and disadvantages in comparison with employed colleagues. In some workplaces it may be easier for those on placement to become part of the team – other team members may value your more independent input to work activity. They may recognise that you bring fresh ideas and welcome you as a participant, remembering also that you may perhaps become a future colleague following your studies. Your participation is seen as fully 'legitimate' – you are seen as a practitioner who is allowed, or entitled, to participate (Lave and Wenger 1991). On the other hand, being on placement may also limit the extent to which you can contribute – your participation may be seen as legitimate only in certain circumstances. There may be certain activities which are 'off limits' and not suitable for you as a novice practitioner. In part, the extent of this legitimation may also relate to how much confidence your colleagues have in you – if you can demonstrate your capabilities in the workplace then you may be more likely to be offered further participative opportunities. Greater discretion and control over your work may be available as you show you are a competent practitioner.

ACTIVITY 2

Think about the following questions:

- In your workplace are there opportunities to participate in a wide range of work activities, and to discuss key concepts with more expert practitioners?
- In which activities are you a 'legitimate' participant?

3 A key model: the expansive-restrictive framework

To help you to identify the character of the workplace you are working in and the potential it offers for learning, we will now explore an adapted version of the 'expansive-restrictive' framework developed by Fuller and Unwin (2004) to analyse learning at work. This framework is useful as it outlines a series of factors that can be identified within workplaces, and points to strategies that could be employed to improve workplace learning for employees. The more 'expansive' factors indicate opportunities for higher quality learning, while the more 'restrictive' factors suggest that workplace learning is more limited and problematic. Only eight pairs of factors are considered here (please see Table 2.1), while the original framework contains 20.

A number of elements of the framework should be emphasised for educational workplaces. First, participating in learning beyond the immediate workplace is important. This may be through involvement in activities with other practitioners in other schools or settings, or perhaps through regional, national or international forums. Equally, the contributions of all colleagues need to be valued, but these colleagues need to be working in a culture that encourages them to work in teams rather than focus only on their specialist roles. This can be difficult if educational organisations are used to operating with staff with highly defined roles and when certain types of expertise are needed. Time away from work for study and professional development is vital for consolidating learning – schools in England hold INSET days for staff development, but there have been questions about whether these are used effectively (Bubb and Earley 2013).

TABLE 2.1 Adaptation of Fuller and Unwin's (2004: 130) expansive-restrictive continuum

Expansive	Restrictive
Participation in multiple communities of practice inside and outside the workplace	Restricted participation in multiple communities of practice
Gradual transition to full, rounded participation	Fast – transition as quick as possible
Planned time off-the-job including for knowledge-based courses and for reflection	Virtually all-on-job: limited opportunities for reflection
Organisational recognition of, and support for employees as learners	Lack of organisational recognition of, and support for employees as learners
Knowledge and skills of whole workforce developed and valued	Knowledge and skills of key workers/groups developed and valued
Team work valued	Rigid specialist roles
Managers as facilitators of workforce and individual development	Managers as controllers of workforce and individual development
Chances to learn new skills/jobs	Barriers to learning new skills/jobs

---

ACTIVITY 3

Comparing workplaces

- Use the expansive-restrictive framework to compare two or more organisations you have worked within or have knowledge of. Which aspects of 'expansiveness' does it seem most difficult to achieve? What stops organisations offering more expansive opportunities to their employees?
- Are all staff contributions recognised and valued in your workplace?
- Do managers facilitate or control individual development?
- How much time off the job do staff have for their development?

---

4 What can we learn from our experience of work?

The focus on context should not allow us to neglect the importance of individual 'dispositions' or attitudes to learning. What you learn from your workplace experience is, to a certain extent, up to you. Opportunities can be made available, but if individuals are not prepared to make best use of them, then learning is unlikely to occur. Billett discusses how 'personal histories' and 'individual agency' can affect which activities are 'judged worthy of participation' (2004, 117), with colleagues deciding to engage with those activities which they perceive as beneficial. There can be 'tension … between the goals of the social practice and those of the individual' (ibid.) in many workplaces if individual members of staff expect opportunities to be available which are not, or if individuals are unable to bring their particular motivations and interests into the activity. In educational organisations there may be considerable differences between the objectives of the organisation and the motivations and interests of staff. Conceptions of the purpose of education are contested, and many current educational initiatives and policies are controversial – the implementation of reform may be perceived as constraining or undermining the interests and values of staff. Although these constraints may seem unsurmountable, there is good reason to think that experienced staff will find ways of working around unpopular reforms to continue to offer the best they can to children and young people. In such cases staff may have to innovate to uphold their values.

For those on placement, there are always opportunities to learn, whatever constraints exist. If opportunities do not obviously present themselves, you may need to use your 'individual agency' to find or create them. It is useful to see the placement as a chance not only to get actively involved in the work of the organisation hosting you, but also to observe how the political and social context shapes the workplace and the learning of your colleagues.

> **ACTIVITY 4**
>
> ■ What is your disposition to learning? How does your personal history shape what you consider to be important to learn and how you react to opportunities? How does this differ from those around you?
>
> ■ What can you do to maximise your learning on placement/in your workplace. List some actions you can take to improve your use of learning opportunities. Discuss these actions with colleagues, asking them for further ideas.

Conclusion

In this chapter you have been introduced to some concepts that underpin how we think about the context of workplace learning that are relevant to those on education studies programmes. The context of workplace learning is shaped by political, social, economic and technological factors and relates both to the culture of an organisation and to how work is organised and managed. It has been argued that forms of participation in workplace activities, supported by an 'expansive' learning environment, are vital for productive learning at work. While it can seem difficult to learn at work in certain contexts, individual agency and motivation are key factors enabling learning to take place.

Follow-up activity

■ Meet with others on your course to compare the environments of the workplaces you have been working in. What are the similarities and differences in term of context and opportunities to learn? What features of expansiveness and restrictiveness are common across workplaces? When was it possible to participate, and when were there constraints? What actions did they take to get the most out of their placement/work environment?

Further reading

Eraut, M. and Hirsh, W. (2007) *The Significance of Workplace Learning for Individuals, Groups and Organisations*. Cardiff: SKOPE.

Griffiths, T. and Guile, D. (2001) 'Learning Through Work Experience'. *Journal of Education and Work*, 14 (1): 113–131.

Rainbird, H., Fuller, A. and Munro, A. eds (2004) *Workplace Learning in Context*. London: Routledge.

References

Billett, S. (2004) 'Learning Through Work: Workplace Participatory Practices'. In Rainbird, H., Fuller, A. and Munro, A. eds *Workplace Learning in Context*. London: Routledge: 109–125.

Bubb, S. and Earley, P. (2013) 'The Use of Training Days: Finding Time for Teachers' Professional Development'. *Educational Research* 55 (3): 236–248.

Eraut, M. and Hirsh, W. (2007) *The Significance of Workplace Learning for Individuals, Groups and Organisations*. Cardiff, SKOPE.

Felstead, A., Fuller, A., Jewson, N. and Unwin, L. (2009) *Improving Working as Learning*. London, Routledge.

Fuller, A. and Unwin, L. (2004) 'Expansive Learning Environments. In Rainbird, H., Fuller, A. and Munro, A. eds *Workplace Learning in Context*. London: Routledge: 126–144.

Handy, C. (1993) *Understanding Organisations*. 4th edn. London: Penguin.

Hordern, J. (2013) 'A Productive System of Early Years Professional Development'. *Early Years* 33 (2): 106–118.

Husbands, C. (2013) 'Great Teachers or Great Teaching? Why McKinsey Got It Wrong' (10 October 2013, IoE Blog) https://ioelondonblog.wordpress.com/2013/10/10/great-teachers-or-great-teaching-why-mckinsey-got-it-wrong/.

Lave, J. and Wenger, E. (1991) *Situated Learning – Legitimate Peripheral Participation*. Cambridge, UK: Cambridge University Press.

National Union of Teachers (NUT) (2012) *Academies Toolkit*. London: NUT. www.teachers.org.uk/files/academies-toolkit-v3-7724.pdf.

Nutbrown, C. and Clough, P. (2014) *Early Childhood Education: History, Philosophy and Experience*. 2nd edn. London: Sage.

Rainbird, H., Munro, A. and Holly, L. (2004) 'The Employment Relationship and Workplace Learning. In Rainbird, H., Munro, A. and Fuller, A. eds *Workplace Learning in Context*. London: Routledge: 38–53.

Penn, H. (2014) 'The Business of Childcare in Europe'. *European Early Childhood Education Research Journal*. 22 (4): 432–456.

Winch, C. (2010) *Dimensions of Expertise: A Conceptual Exploration of Vocational Knowledge*. London, Continuum.

3

The nature of work-based learning on placement

Nick Sorensen

Purpose of the chapter

After reading this chapter you should understand:

- the significance and the nature of work-based learning;
- the importance of reflective practice;
- how learning happens within the workplace;
- how to prepare and plan for your placement in order to get the most out of it.

Introduction

'Why is work-based learning so important?'

An important characteristic of education studies as an undergraduate degree is that it is orientated towards a defined professional arena of environments that are concerned with learning and teaching. Whilst teaching in a formal school setting might be a predominating interest for many undergraduates, there are, in fact, many other contexts where educational activities take place. This can occur in either formal or informal contexts: youth clubs, community centres, museums, drop-in centres. University based courses are enriched through providing opportunities for learning to take place in real life contexts, to supplement and extend the learning that happens within lectures, seminars and tutorials.

We call these opportunities 'work-based learning', a term used to describe 'a class of university programmes that bring together universities and work organisations to create new learning opportunities in the workplace' (Boud 2001: 4).

There is a wide variation in the form of these experiences; from a placement that can last from a single visit to an extended engagement within a professional context that can last over several months where a student might visit the placement for a day a week. An existing course can include experience of a workplace with some work-related assessment activities, or there might be programmes that focus more closely on the needs of learning in work. Whatever the choices that are available, a course that includes work-based learning provides opportunities for new approaches learning and the purpose of this chapter is to outline what these might be and how you can gain the most benefit from them as a student.

The importance of work-based learning is self-evident:

- It provides students with first-hand experience of what it is like to work within a professional context.
- It provides a bridge between what is learnt in the university and the professional practice of the workplace.
- It outlines the relationship between theory and practice.
- It makes the learning in university more relevant.
- It provides experiences that develop professional understanding and knowledge.
- It helps to develop the professional identity of the student, helping them to acknowledge and articulate where they would wish to work within a broad field of educational activity.
- It provides opportunities and experiences of educational work that they might not have previously considered.
- It promotes employability through the recognition and acknowledgement of professional skills and competences.

The nature of work-based learning

ACTIVITY 1

Consider your responses to the following questions:

- What places, other than schools, can you think of where educational activities take place?
- Think about your own experience of school. What examples can you give where learning took place outside of the classroom?
- What do you consider are the most important reasons for engaging in work-based learning?
- How would you want to benefit from work-based learning?

We have seen that there are many reasons why work-based learning is important, but what is the nature of work-based learning? What can be learnt and how is it learnt? What theories does it draw upon? The main area of learning is concerned with experiencing day-to-day life within a professional context. The relationship between a learner and a teacher, youth worker or other professional is complex, and this complexity can never be fully communicated or understood from an outside perspective. We need to experience the world of work in order to fully understand it. A characteristic of all educational activity, wherever it takes place, is that it is unpredictable. No two days are ever the same and that is both a rewarding experience and a challenge for those that work in the sector. Gaining first-hand experience of this is invaluable in its own right but it also provides an opportunity to develop our own professional identity, of being able to acknowledge, and have acknowledged by those in the placement, your emerging professional skills and knowledge. The skills of educators have been developed over a long period of time and consequentially their expertise becomes 'second nature' to them. Work-based learning provides an opportunity to observe and participate in activities in which theory and practice are combined, this is often described as an experiential form of learning.

Experiential learning

Experiential learning has a long and well-defined theoretical tradition that developed in the twentieth century and which acknowledged the importance of learning through experience as opposed to traditional approaches that were centred around the teacher 'transmitting' their knowledge through the medium of lessons, lectures and seminars. Experiential learning emphasises that learning needs to be relevant and connected to the real world. It draws on the foundational theories and ideas of John Dewey (1938) who identified the need for 'forming a theory of experience in order that education may be intelligently conducted upon the basis of experience' as well as others who gave experience a central role in their theories of human behaviour and development: Kurt Lewin, Jean Piaget, Paolo Freire, Carl Rogers and others (Kolb and Kolb 2005).

Drawing on the work of these key figures Kolb (1984) developed an experiential learning theory (ELT). This influential theory provides a holistic view of the experiential learning process and adult development and is based on six propositions.

1   Learning is best conceived as a process (as opposed to being concerned with outcomes), with a primary focus on engaging students in a process that best enhances their learning and includes feedback on the effectiveness of their learning efforts.

2   All learning is relearning. Learning is best facilitated by a process that draws out the students beliefs and ideas about a topic so that they can be examined, tested and integrated with new, more refined, ideas.

3   Learning requires the resolution of conflicts between dialectically opposed modes of adaptation to the world. Conflict, differences and disagreement are what drives the learning process (as) one is called to move back and forth between opposing modes of reflection and action and feeling and thinking.

4   Learning is a holistic process of adaptation to the world. Not just the result of cognition, learning involves the integrated functioning of the total person – thinking, feeling, perceiving and behaving.

5   Learning results from synergetic transactions between the person and the environment. This is a dialectic process of assimilating new experiences into existing concepts and accommodating existing concepts to new situations.

6   Learning is the process of creating knowledge. For ELT this proposes a constructivist theory of learning whereby social knowledge is created and recreated in the personal knowledge of the learner.

(Kolb and Kolb 2005: 194)

Experiential Learning Theory defines learning as 'the process whereby knowledge is created through the transformation of experience. Knowledge results from the combination of grasping and transforming experience' (Kolb 1984: 41), and this is represented as a cyclical activity. Kolb describes this as a four-phase process:

1   concrete experience;

2   reflective observation;

3   abstract conceptualisation;

4   active experimentation.

The cycle portrays two dialectically related modes of grasping experience (concrete experience and abstract conceptualisation) and two dialectically related modes of transforming experience (reflective observation and active experimentation). As Kolb describes it, experiential learning is a process of constructing knowledge that involves a creative tension among the four modes that is responsive to the context in which the learning takes place. The cyclical process involves the learner in engaging in all four of the modes in a recursive (repetitive) process that is responsive to the learning situation and what is being learnt.

Whilst it is possible to engage in the cycle at any point, the ideal starting point is with concrete experience as the key to ELT is active involvement. The assumption is that you cannot learn by simply watching, reading or being told about something, you have to try things out for yourself.

The second stage in the cycle is reflective observation in which the learner steps back from 'doing' in order to review what they have done and what they have experienced. At this point it is important to ask lots of questions and also to engage the others that you are working with. Finding and using the right vocabulary in order to talk about your experience is an important aspect of this mode.

Abstract conceptualisation is the process that learners undergo in order to make sense of their experience. This involves interpreting events and understanding the relationships between them. Comparisons are made between what they have done, what they have reflected upon and what they already know. In the context of work-based learning this may include talking through their experiences back at the university, drawing on research or theory to provide a frame through which they can explain or understand what has happened.

The final stage of the learning cycle is active experimentation, when the learner considers how they are going take their new knowledge and understanding and incorporate it into their own practice. They will be able to adapt and revise the way that they go about handling a task. This final phase of the cycle allows the learner to apply their new knowledge in a context that is relevant and useful to them.

Work-based learning and reflective practice

ACTIVITY 2

Consider your responses to the following questions:

■   Think about an example where you have learnt from experience. What did you learn and how?

■   Analyse your example in relation to Kolb's Experiential Learning Theory. What new insights does this provide?

Kolb's Experiential Learning Theory offers one account of how new knowledge is generated through the process of work-based activities. Central to this approach to learning through doing is the role of reflection. Donald Schön made an important theoretical contribution to way we conceive of reflection within the process of professional learning in his book *The Reflective Practitioner* (1983). He sought to find a more effective way of understanding the intuitive and implicit thinking of professionals than that afforded by 'technical rationalist' accounts, which argues that practice could be improved through the application of scientific theory and technology. This approach is concerned with defining problems and then uses a series of rational steps to solve them.

Schön rejected this account in favour of a more holistic and intuitive approach. He articulated 'an epistemology of practice implicit in the artistic, intuitive processes which some practitioners bring to situations of uncertainty, instability, uniqueness and value conflict'. Schön's view of professional practice is that the knowledge and thought of the practitioner can be seen in the things that they do, in their actions. Professional learning therefore takes place through reflection, and he makes an important distinction between two different kinds of reflection. 'Reflection-on-action' is concerned with looking back on something that has transpired in order to think about its meaning and significance. Contrasting with this is the idea of 'reflection-in-action', reflection that takes place 'in the moment', in the middle of the action.

These ideas have been hugely influential across a number of disciplines including education. Michael Eraut has given critical attention to the notion of reflective practice in his book *Developing Professional Knowledge and Competence* (1994), arguing that Schön's work is more helpfully conceived as a theory of metacognition. Another important book that sets out to reconceptualise and rehabilitate the concept of 'the reflective practitioner' is *The Intuitive Practitioner: On the Value of Not Always Knowing What One Is Doing* (ed. Atkinson and Claxton, 2000).

One of the main problems with Schön's theory is concerned with what is meant by the 'reflection-in-action' and this issue is taken up in a paper by Yanow and Tsoukas (2009). Their view is that Schön's work is essentially cognitivist in nature, that it is concerned with the processes of thinking that occur in the mind of an individual. They see his view of 'reflection-in-action' as sitting back and thinking through a problem after the event, removing himself from what is happening in order to 'think' of another approach.

The cognitivist approach does not give sufficient attention to the fluid and dynamic social characteristics of organisations and the 'spontaneous actions' that feature prominently in organisations (Crossan and Sorrenti 2002: 29). The reality of organisational life is that it consists of flows of interactions that require 'in the moment' responses without interrupting what one is doing in order to reshape our actions and responses. This view draws our attention to the surprises we encounter in any work situation and recognises the importance of improvisation as a significant feature of professional practice. An improvisatory approach to 'reflection-in-action' emphasises that it is embedded (in social activity), engaged (as practice) and embodied (within materials).

'Within such social practices, reflection-in-action is triggered by "backtalk" – surprise – from the materials of the practice, leading the practitioner to improvise a reaction or response' (Yanow and Tsoukas 2009: 1342). Paying attention to the surprises that occur within the workplace draws attention to the processes of continual adaptation and adjustment that take place as people improvise responses to the unexpected within the midst of action. Whilst acknowledging the value of Schön's concept of reflection-in-action Yanow and Tsoukas suggest a more nuanced view that takes into account the improvisatory nature of professional practice.

ACTIVITY 3

■ 'Professional practice is characterised by complexity, is dynamic and interactive and happens in a very specific and constantly changing context' (Atkinson and Claxton 2000: 6). To what extent do you agree with this statement?

■ Cognitivists and social constructionists offer two different ways of understanding the social world based on contrasting assumptions. A cognitivist approach assumes that reality is constituted in the consciousness of the individual mind whilst social constructionists consider that reality is created through social interactions. Consider the differences in these two viewpoints. What assumptions do you hold about social reality?

Work-based learning in a professional masters programme: a case study

We have seen the value of work-based learning within an undergraduate programme in the way that it extends the knowledge and understanding offered in the university setting through providing 'real life' contexts for developing and assimilating professional experience. Many professionals who are working in a wide range of settings wish to extend their learning and gain formal academic qualifications. A Professional Master's Programme (PMP) provides a route whereby they can use their professional experience as the basis for gaining a Masters degree.

Knowledge is accredited through a number of different ways, but what they all have in common is a three-way process by which professional experience is related to relevant research and/or theory and that a critical position is taken towards both professional practice and the theoretical writings. This process is shown in Figure 3.1.

This section provides a case study that outlines an established approach to work-based learning for professionals: action research.

Action research

Samantha is a science teacher who has been working in a secondary school for four years. She already has 60 credits towards a Masters from her Postgraduate Certificate of Education (PGCE), and she feels that she has established herself as a teacher but would like to discover how she can develop and improve her practice further and has registered on a Professional Masters Programme (PMP). She is engaged on a module called Work-based Action Enquiry, and this is based on a research methodology called action research, which is designed to support teachers to improve their own professional practice.

> Action research is simply a form of self-reflective enquiry undertaken by participants in social situations in order to improve the rationality and justice of their own practices, their understanding of these practices, and the situations in which the practices are carried out.
>
> (Carr and Kemmis 1986: 162)

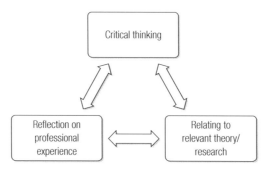

FIGURE 3.1 Engaging with Master's level within a Professional Master's Programme

Action research is a cyclical process, and Samantha based her own project on a five-stage process.

1   She began by deciding on a focus, which was how her teaching could improve the quality of her pupils' scientific explanations. She was particularly interested in supporting her Year 10 pupils.

2   The second phase of the cycle was to find out what was going on already. She undertook an analysis of a sample of Year 10 students' written work and reflected on the strengths and weaknesses of their explanations. She talked to other teachers in the Science Department, but also made the point of talking to teachers in other departments. She undertook some wider reading about the importance of STEM subjects (science, technology, engineering and maths) and literacy across the curriculum. A series of Ofsted reports on the use of language across the curriculum identified writing in science as a weakness that schools needed to address. Finding out that the aspect of her teaching that she wanted to improve was an on-going national issue encouraged her as she realised that the findings of her action research could be of interest to other teachers.

3   Samantha began planning her research and decided that she would try three new strategies to try and improve the quality of pupil explanations in science: developing explanations through the use of keyword definitions; using worked examples; and organising class talk activities to develop written work.

4   Her plans were put into action over a six-week period, and she introduced her three new strategies sequentially. As she was doing this she used different research methods to gather data in order to evaluate the success of her approaches: she handed out questionnaires after each lesson; analysed the written explanations; talked to the students during the lessons and at the end of the six weeks asked a sample of the class to be part of a focus group discussion. During this phase she also wrote down her thoughts and ideas in a reflective journal.

5   The final phase of the cycle was concerned with analysing the data and evaluating the impact of the strategies. She was surprised at the positive impact that class discussion had on written work, giving pupils the opportunity to experiment with ideas before writing them down provided them with greater confidence. An unexpected finding, which came through in the focus group discussion, was that the pupils valued being part of a research process and this in itself was a motivating factor.

Samantha was invited to give a presentation of her research findings at a staff development day, and this became part of the evidence that she presented to her university supervisor for her assessed assignment.

Maximising your learning on a work-based placement

Each placement will be unique as will the individual learning needs of each student. Consequently it is not possible to provide a definitive list to support the planning and preparation for work-based learning. However, the following guidelines will suggest ways in which students can maximise the learning drawing on the case study of action research.

1   Identify your needs: think about the kind of placement that you would ideally wish to go to. What are the benefits of this kind of placement? What might the disadvantages be?

2   Be adaptable: providing placements for students is a challenging process, and the supply of appropriate placements can outweigh the demand. This means that you might not be able to go to your preferred placement. Adapt your plans and needs in the light of the placement that is allocated to you.

3   Research the placement: before you attend for the first time see what you can find out about the placement. Look at their website, read reports about them; find out more about the kind of work that goes on there; identify the professional climate.

4   When you are at the placement negotiate your role and the extent that you can be involved in the professional work. Be clear about the expectations that you have of the placement and what they will have of you. It is unreasonable, for example, for an undergraduate Education Studies student on a placement in a primary school to be asked to teach. However, you may be invited to help with the preparation of a lesson of be asked to listen to some pupils read.

5   Note the 'surprises', the unexpected aspects of the workplace. How do you react to these moments and how do the professionals who work there respond?

6   Keep a reflective diary and regularly find time to record your experiences, responses and thoughts. It may not be possible to do this at the time (this is one of the challenges of reflection-in-action), but after your time in the placement record in as much detail as possible your reflections-on-action.

7   Think about the issues that you encounter and the ways that you react to them? What excites you about the practice that you see? What puzzles you or challenges you? Try and articulate what these issues are and undertake some wider reading about them.

8   Find opportunities to discuss what you are experiencing with as wide a range of people as possible: those working at the placement, your peers, in discussions or seminars at the university. What are you discovering about this example of professional work? And what are you discovering about yourself?

Conclusion

Work-based learning within undergraduate programmes provides an important opportunity to experience the variety and complexity of professional environments. There are opportunities to build and extend the professional identity of the student as they have the opportunity to engage in practical situations. The knowledge generated through work-based learning is heavily dependent on reflection, and we have seen that this knowledge is socially constructed, embedded and embodied, intuitive and improvisational. How we can 'get at' this knowledge can be problematical, although we know it when we experience it.

A well planned placement in which the individual students plays a proactive part in determining what they wish to gain from the opportunities that they have and in which they are encouraged to respond to the unexpected, the surprises of each unique workplace environment can provide a rich opportunity to develop connections between theory and practice, and thereby enrich the university course, as well as clarifying and developing a professional identity that will inform future decisions and enhance employability.

Further reading

Gergen, K.J. (2009) *An Invitation to Social Construction*. 2nd edn. London: Sage. This book provides a valuable and clear introduction to this approach to understanding the social world. Chapter 6 gives an overview of practice-based learning in different contexts.

Sennett, R. (2008) *The Craftsman* London: Penguin. A very readable account of how craftsmen gain their skills through 'doing' and the importance of thinking with our hands.

References

Atkinson, T. and Claxton, G. eds (2000) *The Intuitive Practitioner: on the Value of not Always Knowing What One Is Doing*. Maidenhead: Open University Press.

Boud, D. and Solomon, N. eds (2001) *Work-based Learning: A New Higher Education?*

Carr, W. and Kemmis, S. (1986) *Becoming Critical, Education, Knowledge and Action Research*. London: Routledge.

Crossan, M. and Sorrenti, M. (2002) 'Making Sense of Improvisation'. In Kamouche, K.N., Pina e Cunha, M. and Vieira da Cunha, J. eds *Organisational Improvisation*. London: Routledge: 40–61.

Dewey, J. (1938) *Education and Experience*. New York: Simon and Schuster.

Eraut, M. (1994) *Developing Professional Knowledge and Competence* London: The Falmer Press.

Kolb, D. (1984) *Experiential Learning: Experience as the Source of Learning and Development*. New Jersey: Prentice-Hall.

Kolb, A. and Kolb, D. (2005) 'Learning Styles and Learning Spaces: Enhancing Experiential Learning in Higher Education'. *Academy of Management Learning and Education* 4 (2): 193–212.

Schön, D. (1983) *The Reflective Practitioner: How Professionals Think in Action*. New York: Basic Books.

Yanow, D. and Tsoukas, H. (2009) 'What is Reflection-In-Action? A Phenomenological Account'. *Journal of Management Studies* 46 (8): 1339–1364.

4

Preparing for your placement

Catherine A. Simon

Purpose of the chapter

After reading this chapter you should understand:

- how to choose a placement that is right for you and your course;
- how to negotiate university, placement and personal expectations;
- the value of a reflective journal;
- what to do when things go wrong;
- the practicalities of insurance, health and safety and safeguarding.

A note for international students. Undertaking work-based placements as part of your course is permitted in the UK but is subject to certain rules depending on your status. Your receiving institution should advise you. You can also get information from the UK Council for International Student Affairs: www.ukcisa.org.uk/.

---

1 Introduction: work-based learning in context

The Quality Assurance Agency (QAA) subject benchmark standards for education studies (QAA 2014) recognise the evolution of education studies from its roots in teacher education to a subject in its own right and acknowledge the complexity of defining it as both a 'subject' and as a 'discipline'. Developed as a response to significant changes to UK teacher education in the 1980s, education studies degrees sought to address a perceived lack of critical studies of education contained within the new initial teacher training (ITT) programmes. The subsequent popularity of education studies degrees in the UK – those awards which include early childhood studies, childhood and youth studies, and education studies from a number of national and international perspectives – reflect a continued and growing interest in non-qualified teacher status (non-QTS) pathways for undergraduates in the Higher Education (HE) sector (Palaiologou 2010). Persistent robust recruitment figures to education studies courses in England suggest that the more recent changes to English ITT provision, with the expansion of both routes into teaching and diversity of ITT providers, has not altered this trend.

The QAA define education studies as follows:

> Essentially, education studies is concerned with understanding how people develop and learn throughout their lives, and the nature of knowledge and critical engagement with ways of knowing and understanding. It offers intellectually rigorous analysis of educational processes, systems and approaches, and their cultural, societal, political, historical and economic contexts. Many programmes include the study of broader perspectives such as international education, economic relationships, the effects of globalisation and the role of education in human rights and ecological issues. They all include critique of current policies and practice and challenge assumptions.
>
> (QAA 2014: 6)

Significantly, the QAA acknowledge that 'knowledge, understanding and critical analysis to inform current and future professionals [...] may be achieved through learning in the workplace' (ibid.). The workplace here is not necessarily defined as 'school' and allows for the wider educational experience offered by more informal education settings. These 'alternative' placements may include education-focussed departments or teams within local authorities such as community education, education administration or speech and language services; cultural settings such as libraries, art galleries and museum services (see Chapter 7); or national and local charities and NGOs. They also include settings such as supplementary schools; Pupil Referral Units; youth programmes or after school/out-of-school provision. Some students at Bath Spa, for example, have also negotiated placements within further education (FE) or higher education settings, most commonly working for student support services such as pastoral care; libraries; employability outreach services; or in specific academic departments in support of teaching and learning activities or aspects of curriculum design.

At its simplest, work-based learning (WBL) constitutes learning that is situated in the workplace. The nature and development of that learning resides within a triumvirate composed of the workplace setting, the university and the learner. As measures of employability continue to influence programmes of study in higher education (Speight *et al.* 2012), Lester and Costley (2010) argue that a greater degree of personal self-management and self-direction is required by individuals (in this context the learner) for current and future occupational roles, particularly as the landscape of employment changes. The workplace experience, therefore, is both immediately relevant at a practical level and supportive of the student as a self-managing practitioner and self-directed learner (ibid.).

Nottingham (2011) identified a typology of WBL perspectives: 'discipline' centred; 'employer' centred and 'learner' centred. In the discipline centred model, curriculum design is linked to skills and competencies in the workplace supported by a professional mentor as in the case of ITE, health or engineering. The employer centred model, however, is more closely focussed on workforce development priorities – a model that lends itself to HE accreditation of continued professional development. Finally, in the learner centred model the interests of the learner take priority. WBL is, therefore, not necessarily located in a specific academic discipline but the workplace itself becomes the context for learning. WBL, thus understood, is a transdisciplinary field for the generation of knowledge; one that identifies the generic properties of work and professional practice as a site for academic learning (ibid.). Lester and Costley (2010) consider the most essential component of effective WBL is that which is organised around project based enquiry and permits the learner to address workplace issues. For students out on placement this inevitably means negotiating the complex intersections (boundaries) of applying academic critical engagement to identified issues and understanding the personal and (pre) professional assumptions emerging from the situations encountered.

This requires opportunities for reflection to be built in to any course that provides placement experience for students. Reflection here is understood in a number of ways: in, on and for action. Closely associated with Donald Schön's concept of reflective practice, reflection-in-action suggests practitioners 'know more than they can say' (Dyke 2006: 112), in other words the notion of tacit, instinctive professional knowledge; 'teachers thinking on their feet'. Reflection-on-action, however, refers to the evaluation of one's own practice, as seen for example, in action research paradigms. It is through the process of reflection on practice that workplace experience is transformed into learning (Seibert and Walsh 2013: 168), an approach that emphasises the importance of activity in professional practice such that 'skilful practice may reveal a kind of knowing that does not stem from a prior intellectual operation' (Kinsella 2007: 408), and enables the practitioner to 'examine and evaluate practice in context' (Seibert and Walsh 2013: 168). A useful addition to this simple reflection-on/reflection-in binary, is that of reflection-for-action. This 'anticipatory reflection' (Loughran 1996 cited in Raelin 2011) allows for consideration (prior to the placement experience) of how the learner might approach a given situation. Reflection-in-action then permits the reframing of unanticipated responses, challenging preconceived or underlying/institutional assumptions allowing for the generation of new approaches. Reflection-on-action continues this iterative process.

So how does this apply to selecting and preparing for WBL opportunities?

2 Selecting your placement

One of the benefits of WBL is the opportunity it provides for testing out vocation and skills. Anderson and Mounts (2012) point out that although career exploration is a life-long endeavour beginning in early childhood (ibid.: 91), most adolescents and emerging adults do not explore well their options and possibilities. Accordingly, they point to American research that suggests most university graduates are working in occupations not related to their field of study five years following graduation; it is family and financial considerations rather than career satisfaction that settle those in their late twenties into careers; and 64 per cent of workers would choose another career if they were able to start again (ibid.). It is those in the 18–21 age group, which typically includes university students, who are most likely to be active explorers of occupational identity (ibid.), taking opportunities to try on or try out potential occupations or fields. Allowing time to carefully think through and plan for a placement that will best meet your pre-professional occupational and academic needs will clearly reap benefits for your future.

We have already identified that there are potentially two broad categories of placement associated with education studies – those orientated towards classroom teaching e.g. in school, early years or FE/HE settings – and those broader-based education settings such as cultural industries, charities, local government and education administration. At Bath Spa our Partnership Office liaises with schools to source placements in support of our undergraduate Education Studies and PGCE/ITE programmes. Students seeking other forms of education setting are supported by the careers service. However, the processes involved for students are similar.

2.1 You and your placement: reflection-for-action

It is essential to get your placement right. As in all things careful preparation and research will help you achieve this.

ACTIVITY 1

Consider the following questions:

- What type of placement am I looking for?
- What specific areas of interest are there for you?
- What type of setting will help me fulfil the academic requirements of my module/course?
- What type of experiences will help me develop my knowledge and understanding of work-related practice?
- What skills, competencies and personal characteristics will I bring to the setting?

Answers will depend on a number of factors: your past history and experiences; perceptions of your current and intended skills and competencies; future career aspirations; your character, personal values and beliefs. Answers will also help you identify your personal and pre-professional aims for the placement.

Your placement may well wish to know something about you before you start or you may be required to write a personal statement as part of the application process. Settings need to understand how well you will fit in with an existing team or cope with the challenges of the workplace.

Therefore, try to build up a comprehensive pen picture of the person that is 'you'. We are often our most harshest of critics so it is useful to gain feedback from your peers, family, 'employers'/mentors (if for example you already engage in work or volunteer) and academic tutors. Do not be afraid to promote yourself.

2.2 Be clear about the placement aims

Aims and objectives for the placement will be linked to your specific course or module as well as your personal and pre-professional development aims.

Listed here are the summary aims for students during the placement phase of our core Level 5 module:

STUDENTS SHOULD BE ABLE TO:

- develop coherent knowledge and understanding of an educational topic by making a critical analysis of literature;

- use enquiry methods to carry out the investigation and give an analysis of the methods in relation to their appropriateness for the investigation;

- use professional skills to elicit information and give a critical analysis of the role as an observer;

- gain a coherent understanding of the chosen topic in the context of an educational setting by analysing data from the investigation;

- evaluate the behaviour of learners and/or professionals in a school or other setting, formulate judgements and frame appropriate questions;

- have a critical understanding of the nature of professionalism in educational settings;

- work effectively as part of a team;

- manage their own learning and make decisions about their own work;

- actively organise their own work pattern and work to deadlines.

You should also be aware of the aims of the placement experience for those offering placements. We summarise these as:

- bringing in fresh ideas from a motivated student;

- flexibility of taking students on a short-term basis to help with identified objectives;

- contact with the university leading to joint research projects.

2.3 Sourcing your placement

Your own institution should be able to provide you with guidelines about this. Make use of the Careers Service and Student Union as they have close links with opportunities available in the local area. You can also use networks of family, friends and associates, not to mention students who have taken the course before you, who may have links into the type of workplace you have in mind.

ACTIVITY 2

Researching the employment market

Consider first:

- Do I wish to work in the public, private or voluntary sector?
- Is the potential location restricted e.g. to my term time location, by public transport, distance and travel time?

Then allow time to research the employment opportunities available to you. Consider:

- What are the different roles associated with my area of interest?
- How does my past experience prepare me for a new role?
- What key skills and competencies are employers looking for?
- What are the key skills and competencies I am hoping to develop?

There are a number of web-based sources that may help you. These include:

- www.do-it.org.uk: an excellent website that is easy to use and will help to source placement opportunities.
- www.prospects.ac.uk: A national online careers service providing careers advice and job and course opportunities to students and graduates. There is a designated section to work experience and internships.
- www.milkround.com: Similar to Prospects – will help identify career and training options in education.

Once you have done this and found some potential placements, there are essentially two ways of making contact:

- applying to an advertised opportunity;
- generating a placement opportunity through a speculative application.

Both approaches will require strong and effective letters of application. Again, your institution's careers service should be able to advise you or use the advice pages of online careers services such as Prospects or Milkround. Follow up your initial enquiries by a phone call and/or negotiate a visit. Potential placements are often inundated with enquiries, so the personal touch can go a long way.

2.4 Setting up the placement

In essence you are entering into a semi-contractual arrangement with your placement. This will be set around given expectations i.e. number of days, nature of duties, line management/mentors; pay (if relevant). As such there will be a certain degree of paperwork involved. This may be handled by your institution and should include:

- a statement of roles and responsibilities of the student;
- a statement of roles and responsibilities of the placement provider;
- health and safety procedures pertaining to the placement;
- safeguarding procedures (for placements involving children, young people and/or vulnerable adults);
- information about personal liability and indemnity insurance pertaining to the placement.

Remember, if you are using your own transport during the placement, you should check your personal insurance policy covers you for business use.

3 Negotiating expectations: reflection-in-action

3.1 Before your placement begins

It is good practice to make contact with the placement before the initial start date in order to introduce yourself, meet appropriate staff and raise any questions about the nature of the work, dress code and so forth. If you have any special needs requirements about which the placement should be aware, this is a good time to share them. Often this initial meeting is used as an induction visit. It also allows the placement to check off required paperwork such as DBS (Disclosure and Barring Service) certification and evidence of student status.

3.2 Expectations of students

Roles in the placement should be mutually supportive, and the student's presence should not disrupt the work of the organisation. Your role as a student is to support the organisation as a professional assistant. It is therefore not an expectation that you will simply observe passively but become an active, participant observer. You will, of course, need some time to gain the information required for your academic work, based on the placement experience.

It is expected that you will behave in a professional manner and make positive working relationships with staff and children/young people (if appropriate to the setting).

The following general criteria, therefore may apply to most education studies placements:

- Professional conduct: attendance, punctuality and general conduct in accordance with the professional ethos of the placement (including use of phones and social media); childcare should be well planned in advance with strategies for alternative arrangements if your original child care is unable to cover for whatever reason. Pets may also present an issue for the unprepared. I once had a student leave their placement regularly to walk the dog. The setting did not consider this professional conduct so be prepared to book a dog walker if this applies to you!

- Professional communication with staff, children/young people or vulnerable adults (as appropriate to placement) including social media protocols; find out what is considered appropriate language at the setting, verbal and non-verbal including email protocols.

- Professional relationships with staff: Remember you are joining an already established team.

A note about social media. It is at this point that you may wish to consider very carefully your use of social media. What information would the placement be able to access about you via Facebook, Twitter or Linkedin and the like? Will this be helpful in establishing yourself as a (pre)-professional? Furthermore, how you conduct yourself before, during and after your placement, including evenings and weekends, may be construed as a reflection of your professionalism. What you see and hear on placement is to be treated as confidential (as long as it does not contravene safeguarding policy, in which case you must follow appropriate procedures). It is certainly not advisable to share your thoughts about your placement outside or share your contacts with pupils, children, young people or vulnerable adults.

3.3 Expectations of the placement

The role of the placement is to provide you with the opportunities to work alongside professionals in such a way as to support the development of your pre-professional skills and expertise. To this end the placement may provide you with a mentor who will oversee your work and support you in fulfilling the requirements of your academic work. You should, therefore, be clear about what is required of you, this includes any codes of practice pertaining to the placement. This might be in respect of:

- times of arrival and departure, which should be agreed in advance;
- presentation (e.g. dress);
- use of the placement's social facilities (e.g. staff room, catering);
- use of the placement's learning resources.

If you are not sure, ask.

The placement should also allow you to gain access to the information required for your academic study, but your work should not impose an additional burden on the placement, nor require anything of the placement beyond normal working practices.

3.4 Negotiation

Often there will be a need for negotiation on the part of the student in order to create a balance between the academic expectations for the placement, the practice of professional skills and expertise required by the placement and achieving your personal development goals. Negotiation is an important skill to learn. This means you should be able to articulate your aims and purposes for the placement and employ active listening skills. Your tutor and placement mentor should be able to help you. Clarity, from the outset, is important here for all concerned.

4 Keeping a journal: reflection-on-action

In order to make the most out of your placement experience you are likely to be encouraged to keep a reflective journal. This is a means of capturing your observations, thoughts and ideas *in situ* and allows for reflection after the event. I mention this here as part of preparing for your placement because you will need to consider in advance how you will make notes (electronically or in a traditional note-book), what form those notes will take: written accounts, summaries, pictures; and how you will make use of them to enhance your learning. It is often assumed that we understand what is meant by reflection and reflective practice. Sorensen (Chapter 3) offers some theoretical insights. Further resources on reflection are offered at the end of this chapter.

5 What to do when things go wrong

Sometimes, in spite of the best planning and preparation, the placement does not turn out to be what was expected or things go wrong.

One of the most common issues that emerge from work-based learning is the tension between the academic requirement for critical engagement with your placement and students being critical about professional practices, particularly if they have been highlighted as contested during university sessions. As a student you are in no position, nor are you qualified to make criticisms of the practices you see, even if they do not fit with your knowledge and understanding of professional practice to date, or your own developing sense of professional values and beliefs. Professionals are making themselves vulnerable in inviting students into the placement. Some settings are more used to doing this than others. You should aim to work as partners with your setting in managing and understanding the inevitable conflicts between education policy, theory and practice. Systematically critiquing the intersections of policy, theory and practice and what this means in terms of the lived experience of the placement is one way of avoiding judgemental situations.

If ill health or other circumstances mean that a placement cannot be pursued to completion, you must inform both your setting and your institution of your circumstances. Make every effort to thank the placement for their support to date and leave the door open for another placement opportunity should the need or opportunity arise.

Personality clashes can be difficult. Wherever possible use your professional skills to work around these and keep your focus on the aims and objectives of the placement itself. Even negative experiences can be turned to positive effect.

Wherever there are concerns or worries, be quick to address these through discussion with your academic tutor or placement mentor.

Conclusion

WBL will inevitably challenge your understanding of both theory and practice and may well raise questions for you about the type of professional you wish to be. Preparing for your placement, therefore, is as important as the placement experience itself. The more prepared you are the more likely you will be able to negotiate the complex boundaries between being a student at university and a (pre)professional in the workplace. Systematic reflection for, in and on practice will ease this boundary crossing activity. Establishing clarity over roles and expectations is just one aspect of the process. Understanding the nature of WBL, its links with your university work and its contribution towards your professional development is key. The placement opportunity enables you to explore notions of professionalism and professional identity as well as career profiles and prospects. Practical activities such as writing a personal statement or CV and reflecting on your learning will all contribute to your transition from university into work.

Further reading

There are some useful pages on reflection in the encyclopedia of informal education (infed) (http://infed.org/mobi/writing-and-keeping-journals-a-guide-for-educators-and-social-practitioners/).

Moon, J.A. (2006) *Learning Journals: a Handbook for Reflective Practice and Professional Development.* 2nd edn. Abingdon: Routledge [online]. Available from: http://api.ning.com/files/Sb*4boFSxe NeMU0tE8Zx5vPvWG7Nv2ghBQbodeurTjpDZL7iP8eIEOmFF1oBarmn*WYby*8J38uahT C-gVqdbOlAtZt4GIb-/LearningJournalsAHandbookforReflectivePracticeandProfessional Development2ndEdition.pdf [Accessed 3 August 2015].

References

Anderson, K.L. and Mounts, N.S. (2012) 'Searching for Self: an Identity Control Theory Approach to Triggers of Occupational Exploration'. *Journal of Genetic Psychology* 173 (1): 90–111.

Dyke, M. (2006) 'The Role of the "Other" in Reflection, Knowledge Formation and Action in a Late Modernity'. *International Journal of Lifelong Learning* 25 (2): 105–123.

Kinsella, E. (2007) 'Embodied Reflection and the Epistemology of Reflective Practice'. *Journal of Philosophy of Education* 41 (3): 395–409.

Lester S. and Costley, C. (2010) 'Work-based Learning at Higher Education Level: Value, Practice and Critique'. *Studies in Higher Education* 35 (5): 561–575.

Nottingham, P. (2011) 'An Exploration of How Differing Perspectives of Work Based Learning within Higher Education Influences the Pedagogies Adopted'. PhD. Thesis, Middlesex University.

Palaiologou, I. (2010) 'The Death of a Discipline or the Birth of a Transdiscipline: Subverting Questions of Disciplinarity within Education Studies Undergraduate Courses'. *Educational Studies* 36 (3): 269–282.

QAA (2014) *Subject Benchmark Statement Education Studies: Draft for consultation* [online]. Available from: www.qaa.ac.uk/en/Publications/Documents/SBS-consultation-education-studies.pdf [Accessed 7 August 2015].

Raelin, J.A. (2011) 'Work-based Learning: Valuing Practice as an Educational Event'. In D.M. Qualters, ed. *Experiential Education: Making the Most of Learning Outside the Classroom: New Directions for Teaching and Learning* No. 124, San Francisco: Jossey-Bass.

Seibert, S. and Walsh, A. (2013) 'Reflection in Work-based Learning: Self Regulation or Self-liberation'. *Teaching in Higher Education* 18 (2): 167–178.

Speight, S., Lackowic, N. and Cooker, L. (2013) 'The Contested Curriculum; Academic Learning and Employability in Higher Education'. *Tertiary Education and Management* 19 (2): 112–126.

5

Work-based assessment

Developing new forms of knowledge

Joe Brown

Purpose of the chapter

After reading this chapter you should understand:

- how work-based learning is assessed;
- which key skills and competencies are developed through work-based assessment;
- the value of critical reflection to work-based assessment;
- the nature of collaboration in work-based assessment;
- the ethical requirements governing work-based assessment.

---

1 Introduction: the development of work-based assessment

The last 20 years has seen a significant rise in the number of university-level programmes embedding work-based learning and assessment alongside more traditional pedagogical models (Lester and Costley 2010). These changes have been developed partly in response to demands by both governments and students to make higher education 'work-relevant' in order to address the changing nature of the wider economy and to support accountability agendas (Brodie and Irving 2007). In particular, education studies programmes which have evolved from teacher education often have a strong vocational focus, bringing together theoretical and work-focused knowledge to support the development of current and future education professionals. The Quality Assurance Agency (QAA) Subject Benchmark Statement for Education Studies states:

An education studies programme provides the knowledge, understanding and critical analysis to inform current and future professionals. This may be achieved through learning in the workplace. The subject offers individuals a strong basis for a wide range of further education, training and employment opportunities.

(QAA 2015: 6)

Within this context, work-based or placement-based learning is increasingly being viewed as a way of developing both discipline-specific and transferrable skills within a distinct new site of knowledge (Lester and Costley 2010). Work-based assessment enables students to present this learning, which is contextual, reflective and often collaborative, however, for many 'traditional' higher education (HE) students this form of assessment can be challenging, with the learning often taking place in unfamiliar settings, involving the development of new relationships and requiring competence in inter-personal and self-reflective skills. This chapter aims to support students to recognise the work-based skills and knowledge which are typically assessed and provide advice and support in how to successfully negotiate work-based assessment, whether in employment or as part of a placement.

2 Developing knowledge, skills and capabilities

Traditional concepts of knowledge have often distinguished between theoretical knowledge and the skills and competencies required for specific work contexts. Historically universities taught and assessed theoretical knowledge leaving employability skills to be largely acquired through professional development post-study (Merrill-Glover 2015). Work-based learning and assessment provides opportunities for students to develop both knowledge and practical and transferable skills in new contexts, and explore the links between 'thinking' and 'doing'. This is reflected in the programme outcomes of many university level courses, for example, the Education Studies programme (2015) at Bath Spa University categorises the main learning outcomes as:

1   subject-specific skills and knowledge;

2   cognitive and intellectual skills;

3   skills for life and work.

However, students should be wary of thinking that work-based assessment simply focuses on the development of practical or employment-based skills, or that practice is developed by applying pre-learnt theory. Govaerts and van der Vleuten (2013) argue that work-based learning and assessment is situated within socio-cultural theory where learning is developed through the process of social interaction within specific contexts:

Socio-cultural learning theories therefore consider learning and expertise development to be inextricably linked to features of the context in which the learning occurs; learning processes as well as learning outcomes change as contexts change.

(Govaerts and van der Vleuten 2013: 1166)

This idea of an interdependence between theory and practice means that students need to be clear on the expectations of work-based assessment. In particular, students need to know how work-based learning is assessed, what is being assessed and the attitudes and skills they need to develop in order for it to be successful.

2.1 How is work-based learning assessed?

On most undergraduate programmes the learning requirements are presented through programme or module aims and assessment criteria. Figure 5.1 illustrates a typical relationship between module aims, assessment criteria and assignment titles at undergraduate level.

■ Module aims: Sometimes termed Intended Learning Outcomes, these are the requirements which all students are expected to have met on completion, assessed through the assignments.

■ Assessment criteria: An interpretation of specific module aims which measure a student's knowledge and competence, linked to specific assignments.

■ Assignments: The work which students complete to demonstrate how the assessment criteria have been met, and to what standard.

Before undertaking any work-based assessment, students should understand how these three components link together in order to establish the requirements for specific work-based assignments.

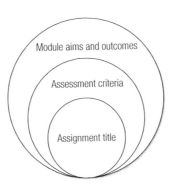

FIGURE 5.1 Components of module assessment

ACTIVITY 1

Study the guide for one of the modules you are undertaking and consider the following:

■ Which of the module aims will be met through learning in a work-based or placement-based context?

■ How are these module aims interpreted in the assessment criteria?

■ Which assignment(s) do these assessment criteria link to?

■ Are there specific work-based or placement-based tasks which I have to undertake to successfully complete the assignments?

Your answers will help you consider the aims and expectations of work-based assignments; what you will need to show you understand and can do; and the tasks you will need to undertake.

Work-based learning is assessed through a wide variety of different assignments, many having distinct aims or areas of focus. Examples of work-based assignments within the Education Studies programme at Bath Spa University include:

■ placement experience;

■ work-based portfolios;

■ assessed professional practice;

■ work-based research or enquiry projects;

■ case studies.

2.2 What is being assessed?

Brodie and Irving (2007) argue that the pedagogy and assessment of work-based learning is focused around three main components, all of which need to be addressed for the learning to be valuable and effective:

■ Learning: Students understand learning theory and approaches in order to maximise the opportunities for their own learning in a work-based context.

■ Critical reflection: Students can critically reflect on work-based experiences and learning and can apply theoretical models to draw conclusions.

■ Capabilities: Students can undertake the practical skills required in specific work-based contexts, such as target setting and interpersonal skills.

This model is broadly reflected in the way module learning outcomes are typically categorised on undergraduate programmes, with many modules on the Education Studies programme at Bath Spa University highlighting three main areas:

TABLE 5.1 Learning outcomes linked to work-based assessment

Outcome category	Knowledge and understanding	Cognitive and intellectual skills	Practical skills
Description	The theories and perspectives students need to know and understand	The skills required for interpreting and presenting knowledge and data	The aptitudes and competencies which support employability
Domain	Subject-specific	Transferable	Transferable and subject-specific
Example	Working knowledge of child development theory	Critical reflection, evidence analysis, structuring arguments	Working as part of a team, communication skills, managing time
Typically assessed through	Essays, reports, research projects	Essays, reflective accounts, research projects	Presentations, placements, observations
Work-based assessment application	*How might my understanding of this theory develop once it is applied to practice?*	*How can I demonstrate the learning which has arisen from work-based experience?*	*How well do I carry out the tasks expected of me in a work-based context?*

- knowledge and understanding;

- cognitive and intellectual skills;

- practical skills.

Table 5.1 provides a breakdown of the different outcomes and their relationship to work-based assessment.

As shown above work-based assessment can contribute to the development of all categories of learning outcomes and provide opportunities to develop both subject-specific and transferable skills and knowledge. Section 3 expands on some of the key skills required for successful work-based assessment.

3 Focusing in on knowledge and skills

Lester and Costley (2010) argue that most work-based assessment is based on the skills of enquiry and research, with students gathering evidence within the workplace to support the development of their knowledge and understanding of key issues within a work-based context. In particular the skills of critical reflection and collaboration are central to successful work-based assessment.

3.1 Reflective skills

Critical reflection is a broad term which is used to describe a number of different activities and is itself part of a wider range of skills Moon refers to 'critical activity', which includes critical reflection, critical evaluation and critical analysis (2008: 27). Within work-based assessment, two forms of critical reflection are crucial:

- Self-reflection: The use of critical reflection to evaluate our own learning and identify future learning needs.

- Reflection for critical analysis: The use of reflection to critique and develop knowledge within a work-based context.

Both these skills are identified within the Subject Benchmark Statement for Education Studies, which states:

> On graduating with an honours degree in education studies, students should be able to demonstrate:

- The ability to reflect on their own and others' value systems
- The ability to use their knowledge and understanding critically to locate and justify a personal position in relation to the subject
- An understanding of the significance and limitations of theory and research.

(QAA 2015: 13)

3.2 Self-reflection

Self-reflection can provide opportunities for students to evaluate their own competence and to question their values and assumptions and the impact they have on practice. In practice this involves a methodical approach which seeks to develop new perspectives and challenge preconceived ideas. The use of a reflective framework such as Schon's reflection-in-action/reflection-on-action highlighted in Chapter 3 can support students to self-reflect in a way that supports professional and personal development.

ACTIVITY 2

When preparing to reflect on your own practice, knowledge or learning ask yourself the following questions:

- What are my personal feelings and values about an aspect of practice and why do I have them?

- Am I prepared to be honest about the limits to my own knowledge and skills?

- Am I willing for my initial thoughts and assumptions to be challenged?

- Am I prepared to change personally and professionally as a result of reflection?

- How will I document my reflection and what framework(s) will I use to do this?

- How will my reflection link to the established theories and research in the discipline I am studying?

3.3 Reflection for critical analysis

Critical reflection is also used as a tool for critiquing theory and knowledge within a work-based context, and students are often asked to link theory to practice in order to form conclusions.

Costley (2007) argues that this link between the theoretical and the technical goes beyond the traditional forms of critical thinking and enables students to develop both transferable skills such as enquiry and analysis and their own practice through ongoing critical reflection. Schon's concept of constructionism places knowledge and action together in an interdependent spiral where the validity of knowledge is 'tested' through practice, generating new knowledge, which in turn affects the way we act (Schon 1987).

ACTIVITY 3

When using critical reflection to critique knowledge ask yourself the following questions:

- How will I use established theory to interpret the evidence gathered – what does this tell me about practice?
- How will I use evidence gathered to evaluate the theory – does theory stand up in the light of practice, or in particular contexts?
- Are my observations and other data consistent with the theories?
- Am I being selective about the data and theory I use in order to create well-argued conclusions?
- Am I being cautious about what my funding mean for wider practice?
- Am I linking my findings to other research evidence on the topic?

The following example shows how critically reflective skills can be embedded in work-based assignments:

EXAMPLE ASSIGNMENT 1

Assignment 2 for the module *'Symbolic Representation: The Foundations of Literacy and Numeracy'* in the third year of the Education Studies programme at Bath Spa University asks students to form conclusions about how literacy and numeracy develop in young children by drawing on both established theory and practice-based evidence in the form of child observations. Students are explicitly directed to link theory to practice and record any unexpected findings, as well as identify the implications for their own practice and understanding.

(continued)

(continued)

Whilst the key focus of this assignment is to support students in generating new knowledge through critical reflection, a number of other transferrable and subject-specific skills and competencies are also developed. For example:

Cognitive and intellectual skills:

- skills of self-reflection;
- skills of evidence analysis;
- skills of academic enquiry;
- developing structured arguments.

Practical skills:

- skills of child observation;
- skills pertaining to ethics – negotiating permission and access;
- communication and collaboration;
- developing autonomy as a learner.

3.4 Collaboration

All work-based learning involves collaboration in some form and students need to be aware of who they will need to collaborate with and for what purpose. Simply attending a placement requires the formation of new relationships with a variety of groups including headteachers and managers, setting staff and children and their families. Work-based assessment requires students to engage in what Costley (2007) refers to as a 'learning partnership' by actively working with staff and other key stakeholders to gather data, test out knowledge and develop their competence. Collaboration also contributes to wider employability skills such as team working and communication.

Students also need to be aware of the impact they can have on others' learning within the work setting. Wenger's idea of communities of practice proposes that practice is improved through the interaction of groups of people who share common aims (Wenger 1999). Where these communities exist the benefits are shared and can lead to improved problem-solving, co-ordination and communication. In reality, work-based collaboration is challenging, involving interactions with unfamiliar people and new work-based expectations. In particular students need to ensure that the collaborative needs of work-based assessment do not negatively disrupt the practice of the workplace.

ACTIVITY 4

When thinking about the collaborative nature of work-based assessment, students should consider the following:

- Who do I need to collaborate with and for what purpose?
- Does the nature of the collaboration depend on my role within the setting, for example, as an employee or a student on placement?
- Are there any work-based expectations for collaborative work, for example, how I communicate with parents?
- What are the opportunities for becoming involved in communities of practice, for example, through staff meetings?
- How do I ensure that the tasks I need to carry out for assessment purposes take account of the needs of others in the setting such as children and staff?
- How will ensure that critical reflection of practice doesn't criticise the setting or other staff?

4 The ethics of work-based assessment

All work-based assessment must be carried out in an ethical manner and adhere to the frameworks and expectations of both the work setting and the university. Within education studies the involvement of children requires a particular focus on ethics governing both working with children and collecting data for assignments. The ethical framework within the Institute for Education at Bath Spa University has been developed from the principles outlined by the British Education Research Association (BERA 2011).

4.1 Ethical principles

- Voluntary informed consent: Students should seek consent from everyone involved in the research, including setting staff and parents. In order for consent to be informed, those involved must be aware of all aspects of the research.
- Openness and honesty: The aims, methods and processes of any research must be fully open and transparent.
- The right to withdraw: Everyone involved has the right to withdraw at any time.
- Confidentiality and anonymity: Steps should be taken to protect the anonymity of everyone involved including children, staff and the setting itself.
- Briefing and dissemination: Students should regularly update those involved in the research and be clear on how who will see it.

4.2 Involving children in work-based assessment

Undertaking work-based assessment which involves children requires a specific set of skills and increasingly children's active participation is seen as a critical element of any enquiry-based project within education. This has in part been influenced by the rise of children's rights and the requirement for children to be consulted and involved in decisions which affect them. Article 12 of the United Nations Convention on the Rights of the Child (UNCRC) states:

> [T]he right [for the child] to express those views freely in all matters affecting the child, the views of the child being given full weight in accordance with the age and maturity of the child.
>
> (UN 1989: 5)

In practice the involvement of children in work-based assessment is focused around two key areas:

- Assent: The term used for the consent of children to be involved in any project. Students need to reflect on how the methods used to seek agreement from children for their involvement are appropriate for their age and level of understanding.

- Active participation: How can students actively involve children in their research, ensuring their voices are a significant part of any work-based project? In particular how can students ensure that the contributions children make provide opportunities to develop their own learning and knowledge.

EXAMPLE ASSIGNMENT 2

In the module 'Professional Practice in an Early Childhood Setting' in the second year of the Education Studies programme at Bath Spa University, students are expected to complete a critical reflection and evaluation of how children learn with data drawn from a portfolio of evidence developed during placement experience. The evidence students gather is a matter of personal judgement but can include observations of children and staff, personal reflections and learning and activity plans and evaluations.

With data potentially gathered from a wide range of documents and activities, an ethical approach to this assignment is crucial. Whilst guidance is given to students about how to seek consent, protect anonymity and feedback to stakeholders, students undertaking this module must also reflect on any specific setting requirements which need to be met, the relationships which need to be developed and how to involve and inform all stakeholders throughout the process.

ACTIVITY 5

When preparing for work-based assessment, ask yourself the following questions:

- What are the ethical requirements outlined in the module guide?
- Are there any specific templates or forms required to gain ethical approval before I start the project?
- Are there any ethical requirements or procedures within the work or placement setting which need to be met?
- Who do I need to collaborative with in other to meet ethical requirements?
- How do I ensure that all parties are kept up to date and information is shared with them throughout the project?
- What information do I need to include to ensure consent is fully 'informed'?
- What methods will I use to seek children's assent and involve them in the project?

Conclusion

This chapter has outlined how work-based learning is assessed on undergraduate programmes and discussed some of the key skills which work-based assessment aims to develop. Students should be aware that work-based assessment is wide-ranging, not only supporting practical and employability skills but key intellectual skills such as analysis, reflection and the application of knowledge in specific contexts. However, work-based assessment should also be approached with an understanding of the impact students can have on the staff, children and their families in educational settings and how this can be addressed. In particular students should view work-based assessment as an opportunity to develop personally, reflecting on how they think, behave and interact in professional situations with a view to understanding their own strengths and areas for development and inform their future career aspirations.

References

British Educational Research Association (BERA) (2011) *Ethical Guidelines for Educational Research*. London: BERA.

Bath Spa University (2015) *Definitive Programme Document, Education Studies*. Bath: BSU.

Brodie, P. and Irving, K. (2007) 'Assessment in Work-based Learning: Investigating a Pedagogical Approach to Enhance Student Learning'. *Assessment and Evaluation in Higher Education* 32 (1): 11–19.

Costley, C. (2007) 'Work-based Learning; Assessment and Evaluation in Higher Education'. *Assessment and Evaluation in Higher Education* 32 (1): 1–9.

Govaerts, M. and van der Vleuten, C. (2013) 'Validity in Work-based Assessment, Expanding Our Horizons'. *Medical Education* 47: 1164–1174.

Lester, S. and Costley, C. (2010) 'Work-based Learning at Higher Education Level: Value, Practice and Critique'. *Studies in Higher Education* 35 (5): 561–575.

Light, G. and Cox, R. (2001) *Learning and Teaching in Higher Education: the Reflective Professional.* London: Paul Chapman Publishing.

Merrill-Glover, K. (2015) 'Working Towards Powerful Knowledge: Curriculum, Pedagogy and Assessment in Work-based Learning'. *Widening Participation and Lifelong Learning* 17 (1): 22–37.

Moon, J. (2008) *Critical Thinking, an Explanation of Theory and Practice.* Abingdon: Routledge.

Quality Assurance Agency (QAA) (2015) *Subject Benchmark Statement, Education Studies.* London: QAA.

Schon, D. (1987) *Educating the Reflective Practitioner.* San-Francisco: Jossey Bass.

United Nations (1989) *UN Convention on the Rights of the Child.* London: Unicef.

Wenger, E. (1999) *Communities of Practice, Learning, Meaning and Identity.* Cambridge: Cambridge University Press.

Issues and case studies of placement and work-based learning

Introduction

Section B

Catherine A. Simon

So far we have outlined the theoretical and practical aspects of work-based learning in the context of education studies. This next section of the book explores in more depth the lived experiences of students engaged in work-based learning in a broad range of educational settings. Through a series of case studies we consider the nature and purpose of placements in different contexts and the issues these raise for undergraduates and their tutors. Examples are drawn from both local and international placement experiences, and extend across a broad range of educational settings. Central to the case studies which follow is the student and their experiences of negotiating the various roles of academic learner, pre-professional and active practitioner in the workplace. These experiences can be summarised in terms of challenge, change and collegiality.

Challenge

A core theme to emerge from the case study examples is that of challenge. We see students challenged in a variety of ways: in terms of their understanding and beliefs about theory and practice; their preconceived ideas and stereotypical views of professionals and learners in a variety of contexts; and finally about their own professional aspirations and future career identity. Empowerment is seen as part of challenge. June Bianchi's examples of cultural placements (Chapter 7) demonstrate the potential for 'cultural institutions [to] ... contribute towards personal empowerment, challenging socio-economic exclusion'. Student engagement with such institutions leads to personal empowerment, as Bianchi's example of Rondene Vassal powerfully illustrates. The theme of challenge and empowerment is also evident in Laura Green's case studies (Chapter 11). Empowerment underpins much of youth and community work, and whilst students are exposed to youth and community projects they not only see how such work challenges oppression and inequality in the lived experiences of others, but they also have the opportunity to consider the impact of their own life choices on those of the more disadvantaged. Students are thus able to consider how this might frame the values and interventions considered best for young people and their communities.

Challenging stereotypical views and normative perceptions can also be seen through the school based examples provided by Richard Riddell (Chapter 6), where complexity in terms of classroom context, theory and practice presents a particular level of challenge. Not only do unqualified, emergent academic undergraduates have to make sense of government policy, expectations for schools and schooling and particular notions of professionalism held by a range of stakeholders, they also have to navigate the complexities of schools as institutions, and the individual histories that brought them to a decision to pursue teaching as a career. The potential disconnect between students' life experiences, university study and the requirement to critique, using theory and research, the strong norms presented by classroom practice, is also pertinent here. As tutors and student observers it may well be possible to conclude that a child's reticence to perform certain tasks was because they possibly were too challenging or the child did not want to be seen as failing, but in no way can we be sure this is a reasonable explanation nor should we be too quick to make such assumptions.

Students can also find their stereotypical views and preconceived ideas questioned when they engage with different cultures and unfamiliar contexts. This is particularly true of overseas placements. Lone Hattingh (Chapter 8) and Dan Davies (Chapter 10) present clear accounts of student responses to the unfamiliar. For students on a field trip in Denmark, a culture of outdoor learning confronted our English students' preconditioning about risk and health and safety. Similarly 'Simon's' experience of Zambia uncovered some stereotypical beliefs around poverty and culture, which led to mature reflection on what he encountered in reality. Indeed as Davis observed, these opportunities can lead to 'different kinds of learning from those associated with the university-based module' to which the international placement was linked.

Change

Challenge, therefore, in many instances, can lead to opportunities for change in terms of thinking, assumptions, expectations and practice. Mary Dooley's chapter on working with students with specific learning difficulties (Chapter 9) demonstrates how students can be opened to viewing issues of dyslexia through 'an affirmative' lens, which can expose learners' strengths rather than focusing on perceived weaknesses. Indeed, reflection is often the key to unlocking and understanding new perspectives and the notion of reflection either on, in or for practice, runs through all of the case study chapters. Martine Duggan (Chapter 12) explores how reflection on everyday experiences during work-based learning in early years settings can underpin academic study. The intersections between critically reflective and analytical practices of early years professionals and the academic nature of critical thinking and criticality make the barriers between the academic and practical more permeable. This demands a degree of support and collaboration between the student, the practitioner and the academic tutor.

Collaboration

Indeed collaboration – with peers, with learners, with professionals and with university staff – underpins our values about learning and knowledge production. Hordern (Chapter 2) refers to the work of Billett (2004) and the concept of participation in the social world. Such participation involves interaction with professionals such that students can make sense of the workplace and workplace practices. Students therefore may be joining a 'community of practice' such that they become participants in, as well as observers of, the social world of the setting or educational institution. As indicated earlier, we have to be mindful of the judgements that students (as novice pre-professionals) and tutors may make, and be careful to link these to academic study. In this way collaboration with professionals should be seen as providing opportunities for the co-construction of knowledge rather than viewing the professional and the workplace as 'subjects' or 'objects' in a knowledge production enterprise. Collaboration with practitioners guards against this.

Peer to peer collaboration is also important for work-based learning programmes and placement opportunities. Students may be encouraged to share their experiences during seminars or via online blogs or discussion boards. It may be possible for students in school-based settings to engage in paired placements, where they can work together in a classroom setting, sharing notes, activities, discussions with staff and personal reflections. This adds richness and depth to the experience and allows students to view the same situation through another person's eyes.

It is here that the role of the academic tutor or seminar leader can be particularly useful in guiding students towards appropriate reading, theory or research. Indeed it is through reflection and collaborative learning and practice that students are able to develop as learners and adults in the real world. The whole points to work-based learning as an instantiation of transformational learning (Mezirow 1997). In essence the following chapters offer good examples of this process, one which:

> involves transforming frames of reference through critical reflection of assumptions, validating contested beliefs through discourse, taking action on one's reflective insight, and critically assessing it.
>
> (Ibid.: 11)

One final point to note through the case studies which follow is the celebration of good practice, hard work and professionalism not only displayed by undergraduates but also on the part of all those who have welcomed students into their everyday world of work. We are unable to capture in the pages of this book the full extent of these student encounters nor the richness of their stories and the insights they bring back to the seminar room. Educationalists' professional practice is often open to scrutiny, either by peers as part of routine staff development, through Ofsted or other formal inspection processes, evaluation, parent partnership and engagement with the very children and young people they encounter daily. To be willing to invite students into this mix adds another dimension of responsibility and expectation to a workload which we do not take for granted nor undervalue.

References

Billett, S. (2004) 'Learning Through Work: Workplace Participatory Practices'. In Rainbird, H., Munro, A. and Fuller, A. eds *Workplace Learning in Context*. London: Routledge: 109–125.

Mezirow, J. (1997) 'Transformative Learning: Theory to Practice'. *New Directions for Adult & Continuing Education* 74 (1): 5–12.

6

Placements in schools and other educational settings on a core undergraduate module

Richard Riddell

Purpose of the chapter

After reading this chapter, you will:

■ understand better the differing roles of placements in undergraduate degree courses in education;

■ be acquainted with the placement provision as part of the degree programme run at a case study institution (Bath Spa University);

■ have begun to think about what you can yourself get out of a placement in an education setting.

Background to placement: undergraduate study programmes in education

Bath Spa University's BA and BSc programmes in Education Studies are examples of what Furlong (2013: 75) describes as 'mainly academic' degree courses 'that have flourished in recent years'. They have evolved from earlier, often BEd degrees, which were sometimes seen by their host universities as 'tips for teachers' (Ward 2012), but combined a degree with qualified teacher status (QTS). Universities began to consider a deeper theoretical element was necessary in return for continuing accreditation at degree level, and hence the evolution of these newer recent degrees.

An advantage of such courses to the staff teaching them is that they are able to sidestep the 'intensive government prescription and scrutiny' that courses preparing teachers are subject to (ibid.: 75). Numbers have proved buoyant, as Furlong also says, and Bath Spa has been able to recruit strongly in recent years, including by surpassing the previous cap for 2016/17.

Many students undertaking such a degree, albeit still a minority, no longer see teaching as their career goal. As the Bath Spa handbook says, the degree will:

> provide an excellent preparation for you to work with learners of all ages within the education sector. The commercial and industrial worlds are also very interested in people with knowledge about education and training. You will have the knowledge and skills to work in educational and training advisory roles in a range of organisations including businesses, local authorities, non-government organisations, charities, museums, art galleries and libraries.

The course handbook also explains that the degree can be the basis for applying for PGCE or other courses leading to Qualified Teacher Status (QTS). Education studies has thus become a degree 'subject', no longer tied to a particular destination, even within the various professions involved with schools and the wider education service.

Parallel to this, initial teacher professional preparation for teaching has taken more of a 'practical turn' since the 1980s, as Furlong says, and according to most recent government policy needs to be rooted in classroom experience (Carter 2015). It is now once again termed initial teacher training as opposed to education.

The clear bifurcation of academic study and training in education hence entail the multivalence of placements taken as part of undergraduate study. For students considering teaching as a career, this is an additional placement experience to observe and prepare themselves for teaching and the additional academic qualification, as Carter calls it – the PGCE – that is one route to QTS. For this course, students are generally expected to have had at least two weeks placement in a school before applying for it. The current alternative employment and school-led routes to QTS are set out at www.getintoteaching.education.gov.uk.

At the same time, by the time students approach the placement they are half way through the academic studies for their degree. They have studied modules both intended to introduce them to the major disciplines involved in studying education – for example philosophy, history, psychology, sociology – and modules concerned with specific aspects of educational provision, such as early years, the primary classroom, literacy, numeracy, children with additional support needs, adolescence, assessment, globalisation and how these are all shaped by policy. Irrespective of intended career destination, the placement provides an opportunity to observe and interpret educational or other practice on the basis of what they have learned to date without the complication of being responsible for children.

Further, as schools and other settings in England represent an instantiation of long-standing detailed national policy direction – heads and teachers are 'enactors' of policy (Ball *et al.* 2012) and are positioned by it (Gunter 2012) – students can begin to understand how provision shapes the early lives of children and young people, with long-term consequences for the shape of our society and the inequities of English social reproduction. For this particular phenomenon they are not just being made aware, depending on the tutoring, of an aspect of professional practice in isolation from every other social process that may be occurring or being formed in the room or school more widely.

The shape and place of the placement

The Education Studies core year 2 module in its current manifestation – at the time of writing it was being prepared for the internal periodic review by the university – is in three distinct phases. The first term of 10 or 11 weeks is taught through a combination of a weekly one-hour lecture and a two-hour seminar to follow up and discuss the issues it raises. The lectures cover some general topics such as the nature of policy, the shape of schooling in England, progression to and participation in education and training post-16, marketisation and its effects, inclusion – with particular reference to the recent SEND (special educational needs and disability) reforms – and inequality, including the particular inequities by gender, race and class. The lecturer leading each week provides materials for tutors to use in the seminars. The emphasis in these lectures differs from year to year depending on current developments, but they are intended to provide students with the background to current 'issues' or controversies in education and the academic tools to analyse them *in situ*.

Students are asked to consider the placement they would like at the beginning of the first term, and are asked to state any particular preference they may have for phase or sector to accord with their interests or professional preferences at that stage.

There are two written assignments for the first term of the module. The first is an assignment in data analysis, comparing outcomes between schools, countries or post-16 participation. Students are expected to reflect not just on what the data signify, but the why behind the phenomena they exemplify. The second assignment is a more traditional essay of 2500 words. This provides an opportunity for students to explore academically some of the matters discussed during the first term, chosen from a list provided in the handbook. Together, these assignments carry 50 per cent of the marks for the module.

The placement takes place in the spring term and consists of a full day a week for ten weeks. This may be slightly modified depending on the calendar, specifically when Easter occurs and the spring term is shorter.

There are additional preparatory lectures concerning research methods, specifically an introduction to ethnography intended to give the students some idea of how to research and reflect on a setting in which they live semi-professionally as an active participant. At the same time, they are given a picture of the contemporary English classroom with its multiple professional and sub-professional roles and the sorts of leadership activities they may observe.

The module handbook explains that the 'placement is intended to enable you to study in some detail an educational topic in an education setting' and that a principal purpose of the placement is to 'carry out an investigation', including a 'critical analysis of a range of policy issues relating to your education setting'. These are intended to lead to the writing of a 5000 word report that counts towards 50 per cent of the marks for the module.

Support for the students on placement and its follow up is provided through up to four seminars that take a variety of workshop formats – sharing experiences, writing a literature review, observation skills, how to write up findings and how to discuss them – and a series of one-to-one tutorials with the seminar tutor. These take place at strategic points in the process of researching and writing the report, beginning with help in narrowing down the choice of the topic at the beginning of the spring term and suggesting readings. The tutors do not visit the students on placement – in this sense it is not supervised.

In one of the first seminar workshops, students are encouraged to think about their own goals for the placement in terms of their professional and personal learning. They then review and reflect on these in the final seminar/workshop and prepare a short presentation of their own skills, attributes and knowledge within the context of employability. For many students, this is the first opportunity to do this during their undergraduate career.

ACTIVITY

Think about the placement(s) you have undertaken or are about to take as part of your course. What professional skills would you like to develop? How could you use the opportunity of being in the workplace to deepen your understanding of the processes involved?

What the students can gain

The placements undertaken by students include early years settings and primary, secondary and special schools, sometimes including those in the private sector. As might be expected, the range of placements has expanded further in recent years taking in voluntary organisations (e.g. the Red Cross), charities and youth work settings, reflecting the wider student interests on the degree course. So students may be expected to learn different things.

The following discussion of what benefit students are able to take from the placement are based largely on my own experience as a tutor for six years on the course, during which time I have given regular lectures, taught ten seminar groups and provided tutorial support to over 120 students, marking all their assignments. My observations are no doubt therefore selective though they are leavened by discussions at a variety of course and moderation meetings over the years, largely face to face but more recently on line.

To begin with, there are two sorts of learning while on placement that potentially can be in conflict. The first involves bringing their academic studies and a variety of analytical tools to bear on the spoken, observed and documented reality of the settings in which they are placed. Students at Bath Spa are encouraged to be reflective in their work and conclusions, in accordance with the QAA Education Studies 2015 benchmarks, and to think critically about their experience and more generally. This does not mean being openly critical while being on placement, of course, even with the advantage of a fresh pair of professional eyes, but I have had a number of what I sometimes think of as 'OMG Conversations' over the years with students in tutorials whereby they express their disbelief – personal, academic and sometimes stridently expressed – at practices they have observed. Recent examples have included the seating behind a bookcase (out of sight of the class teacher) of a child assessed as being on the autistic spectrum in a Year 1 class in a school repeatedly considered outstanding by Ofsted, and with a model inclusion policy. Another has been the operation in a Year 4 class, again in another well-thought of school, of what in fact are unchanging streamed groups for all subjects, with the accompanying problems of self-identification and self-concept for the children. Finally, a student pointed out in her placement school what has become a more observed commonplace (Blatchford et al. 2012) concerning the use of teaching assistants (TAs) in classrooms: children with identified mild or severe SEND spend their time with the least qualified member of staff in the room while the teacher may spend most of her time with the 'top group', whose data were vital to the school until more recent changes in the assessment (and inspection) of progress.

There are a variety ways of discussing this with students in tutorials to help them think about it. First, the student can be encouraged academically to ensure they have gathered the full picture behind what they are observing before coming to a conclusion: do the arrangements for children vary for example; have they been asked for their perceptions; what does the school policy say and how is it justified; how does the class teacher explain the strategy and see the benefits for the children; and what are the SENCO's (special educational needs coordinator) and headteacher's points of view? Further, what is the research saying? These are all useful ways of encouraging the development of informed reflection about what is happening to children that is desirable – in teaching and no doubt other professions – but also in being a good citizen.

Second, however, the broader professional skills can be explored: how will the student fit into a professional community? I have encouraged students to think about earning the right to challenge – important for any future classroom or indeed leadership role in any setting. Do they know and have they seen enough to justify their conclusion? Do they speak with any authority and would anyone listen? Should they? So the students learn to be critical, but not necessarily openly. This may then result, however, in findings that are not shared with the school and its staff, creating an ethical conflict in research terms. So there are fairly deep issues to be worked through with the student, including how to be judicious and professional while not necessarily keeping quiet or accepting practice unsupported by evidence.

Although we have not systematically kept a record of the students' self-assessment of the skills and understanding they have developed over the placement, there are several common ones that come up time and again. First, with regard to a career in teaching, students variably discover or rediscover why they had made a commitment when quite young to become teachers. For some students the placement is truly transformational – their experiences are described as inspirational, sometimes because they have been given responsibility for quite large groups of children (occasionally a whole class) and have received a glimpse of the possibility of their being empowered and effective professionals. One recent student changed her career aspiration from librarianship saying 'nothing could be as important as teaching, making a real difference to children's lives'. For others, the placement can have the opposite effect when they have seen at first hand the complexities in diverse classrooms that teachers try to reconcile in order to ensure effective learning and progress, and the amount of commitment and hard work this entails.

But even this empowers some. Another recent student on the inclusion pathway of the degree, described how 'on my Education Studies journey, I have grown to understand that some pupils … [in] a mainstream or a special school, may have problems in accessing the curriculum due to their learning difficulties'. Her placement in an all-through special school for children with 'a variety of complex learning difficulties' gave rise to a micro-study of the use of various ICT and IWB-based (interactive white boards) applications to assist students' learning – hugely indicative of the affordances that teachers employ and the practicality of working with children. The appreciation of such practicalities by repeated observation while not yet being responsible for children gives potential teachers some preparatory understanding of how classroom strategies can be implemented and monitored before they have to do it for themselves.

Other students gain from seeing and being part of unimagined worlds. At one end of the spectrum, a student by no means from a deprived background was placed in the primary department – in a Year 4 class – of a prestigious independent school close to the university. She was taken aback by the competitiveness of the children in the classroom (eight year olds): for example, vying for first place in class tests and being told by one girl she spoke to who was interrogated by her parents on why she had only come second in a regional instrumental competition.

At the other end of the spectrum students are placed in a variety of schools serving disadvantaged areas across the south west. Many of these communities have been disadvantaged for some time, but their context has become more complex with the effects of migration in recent years – schools I knew well formerly as white working class schools had become substantially multi-ethnic and multi-lingual. Bath Spa students themselves do not come from particularly disadvantaged backgrounds and the university is close to benchmarks for its admissions in recent years. For example, against a national average of universities from all mission groups of 32.6 per cent of students being admitted in 2013–14 from NS-SEC (National Statistics Socio-economic Classification) categories 4–7 (the closest this classification gets to working class), 34.6 per cent of students were admitted to Bath Spa. And 93.1 per cent of students admitted for the same year attended state schools, about the same as the national average. (Statistics available at www.hesa.ac.uk/pis/summary1314.)

So some placements have provided shockingly new and different experiences. One student was placed in a large primary school serving a local authority housing estate that had seen better days. In fact, it was not far from the student's own home. She was surprised in a reception class by how little communication, if any, took place between parents and the staff at the beginning and end of the day and the preliminary rudeness of a boy she was working with. I have commented elsewhere (Riddell 2003) on the 'negative honeymoons' experienced by staff at all levels in such schools until both parents and children become more accustomed to them. Luckily for this student, the boy she named Tom eventually accepted her, although he still, even at this stage of his career, refused to do certain tasks, either because they were perceived to be too challenging or he did not want to be seen to be failing.

But also for this university student, her reflection on how the staff talked about Tom led to a period of profound reflection on the role of schooling. A TA, after the student's surprise at being struck on the legs by Tom on her first day, had described how she herself had just 'got used to it'. Her response to Tom's behaviour was to 'give him space' and hold him up as an example of 'how not to behave' to the other children. Further, a teacher described how she felt 'insulted' by new attempts in the school to improve the quality of children's experiences. Those of them who had 'been [there] for years' she said felt 'they knew them better than anyone'.

As the student said, she felt 'the school has moulded itself into the deprived community'; it was a reflection of the 'society it is situated in'. Parental unwillingness went 'unchallenged'. So the way expectations of children were moulded at this stage of their lives helped maintain current social inequalities. This is a profound connection between the micro-processes of classrooms and the wider structure of society.

Another student experienced similar complexity in the urban classroom she was visiting, so she painted a convincing narrative portrait of it. She examined the interplay in this classroom between migration and inclusion policy, speakers of English as an Additional Language, speech impairments, emotional and behavioural difficulties and the 'ability-based' classroom management, while the needs of high ability children appeared to be neglected. She considered how the teacher, who stated her role as 'closing the gap', attempted to integrate modified classroom approaches to meet the needs of particular groups of children into a coherent whole, while the TA felt 'overwhelmed' sometimes by the behaviour. This particular student saw the solution in the form of a more flexible curriculum.

Both these latter students had managed to make sense of complexity in the presenting context of these classrooms while beginning to understand the difficulty of designing the appropriate professional responses required and remaining enthusiastic about becoming teachers. Both – and many of their peers – had begun to bring to bear a wide variety of published research evidence, either recommended by the tutor or discovered themselves – to the reality they were experiencing. At the same time, they were being challenged to think about the limitations to the conclusions they could draw or recommendations they could make, rooted in evidence. At a time when schools and the teaching profession more generally are being asked to consider the relevance of research to their classroom practice, ranging from large-scale randomised control trials to the micro-studied irreproducible results of action inquiry, this is a perfect combination of mature study and reflective professional observation and preparation.

Further activities and reading

In relation to preparation for teaching, it is worthwhile reading both Chapters 5 and 6 in the Furlong book listed alongside the Carter review.

Consider how teachers – and other professionals – are positioned by external agencies' expectations of their work – with which they do not agree – and yet remain enthusiastic and committed. How will this work for you, whatever your career destination?

For developments in integrating research into schools, read the contrasting Chapters 1 and 2 in Chris Brown's book below.

Acknowledgements

I would like to thank my students from all the Ed 5001 seminar groups I have taught for their reflections on the course and their placements, and for the permission given by students on the 2014/15 course to quote their placement reports.

References

Ball, S., Maguire, M. and Braun. A. (2012) *How Schools Do Policy. Policy Enactments in Secondary Schools.* London: Routledge.

Blatchford, P., Russell, A. and Webster, R. (2012) *Reassessing the Impact of Teaching Assistants. How Research Challenges Practice and Policy.* Abingdon: Routledge.

Brown, C. ed. (2015) *Leading the Use of Research and Evidence.* London: Institute of Education Press.

Carter, A. (2015) *Carter Review of Initial Teacher Training (ITT).* London: DfE.

Furlong, J. (2013) *Education – An Anatomy of a Discipline. Rescuing the University Project?* London: Routledge.

Gunter, H. (2012) *Leadership and the Reform of Education.* Bristol: The Policy Press.

Riddell, R. (2003) *Schools for Our Cities – Urban Learning in the 21st Century.* Stoke-on-Trent: Trentham Books.

Ward, S. ed. (2013) *A Student's Guide to Education Studies.* 3rd edn. London: Routledge.

7

Cultural placements

A sense of self, a sense of place

June Bianchi

Purpose of the chapter

After reading this chapter you should understand:

- key perspectives, policies and theoretical approaches to cultural experiences and institutions;
- the significance of cultural placements in disseminating diverse perspectives on culture and society;
- the role of cultural placements in enriching participants' sense of self and sense of place within a changing society;
- the impact of a cultural placement on educational and career development.

Introduction

'What is your experience of culture?'

This open-ended and ambiguous question, inevitably elicits discussion not only in relation to what 'culture' is but also where it takes place. Family backgrounds, food culture, family and community rituals, social and religious observances are frequently cited alongside experience as audiences and participants within educational and cultural institutions and settings. Culture is defined as 'ideas, customs, and social behaviour of a particular people or society' (Oxford Dictionaries: undated), and cultural theorist Williams observed that human societies express cultural meanings and purposes 'in institutions, and in arts and learning' (1958, cited in Higgins 2001: 11). Cultural institutions and settings therefore occupy a key role in generating and disseminating cultural perspectives and practice, providing public access to a diversity of visual, performance-based and interdisciplinary arts.

Whether exploring personal interest, investigating potential employment prospects or developing transferable skills, cultural placements provide a focus for enriching and developing a sense of self in relation to a wider sense of place. This can incorporate a range of cultural perspectives and contexts: historical and contemporary; local, national and international; traditional and innovative; institutional and community-based, facilitating deeper understanding of the roles fulfilled by a cultural setting:

- generating publicly accessible cultural productions;
- promoting and validating featured art-forms;
- raising issues through the arts;
- engaging with audiences and participants.

Placements provide an empirical context for critical reflection on the wider educational significance of cultural institutions and settings in relation to lifelong learning.

Culture experience and institutions: an overview

ACTIVITY 1

Consider your responses to the following questions:

- What access did you have to cultural experiences, institutions and settings within your family, social and educational environment?
- What factors enabled or limited your access?
- To what extent has your cultural access widened as an adult?

While some form of cultural participation is integral to every child's upbringing, access to cultural institutions is informed by economic and social factors, many inequitable. International research data, published in France in 1969 (Bourdieu and Darbel 1991), established that the composition of museum and gallery audiences reflected the social, cultural and economic capital of their family, with visitors predominantly professional, university-educated and affluent. Despite apparent democratisation of cultural production and access, such audience profiles still predominate in the twenty-first century (Department for Culture, Media and Sport 2014). While the Arts Council promotes everyone's right to visit 'a high quality museum, library or live performance or participate in a cultural activity' to stimulate 'reflection, engender debate and critical thinking, and deepen our understanding of the world' (Arts Council England 2013: 28), it nevertheless expresses concern that arts investment predominantly benefits society's most privileged.

Current data indicates that arts engagement remains, as previously, highest amongst upper socio-economic groups, with levels of 82.4 per cent participating in an aspect of arts and heritage compared with 66.5 per cent in lower socio-economic groups. Correspondingly, arts and cultural participation of black and minority ethnic (BME) groups is 67.2 per cent compared with 72.2 per cent within equivalent white groups, 78.6 per cent of well adults participated in comparison with 72.2 per cent with long-term illness or disability, while the engagement of 80.3 per cent of working adults compared with 71.1 per cent unemployed (DCMS 2014). Cultural hierarchies reinforce status within society, disenfranchising the socio-economically and educationally deprived, and emphasising 'for some the feeling of belonging and for others the feeling of exclusion' (Bourdieu and Darbel 1991: 112). Cultural institutions, as recipients of public funding, hold responsibility to provide worthwhile experiences for all stake-holders; taxpayers form part of this group alongside cultural organisations like the Arts Council, local authorities, individual benefactors, charitable and educational foundations. Yet cultural spending is an unequal form of distribution; alongside considerations of socio-economic and cultural capital, geography represents a key access and provision factor within the arts. 2012–13 Arts Council England data indicated allocations of £21.90 per capita within London, compared with an average of £8.23 per capita in the rest of England, a figure aggregating the lowest allocation of £3.25 within the South East (Arts Council Spend Per Head, 2013b).

Access to cultural experience signifies confidence and self-esteem, bestowing status and value in tandem with social, educational and economic capital (Bourdieu 1989). While cultural capital can engender entitlement, reinforcing social hierarchies and imbalances of power, it can also challenge privilege, generating new opportunities for those traditionally excluded. International data gathered in 2011, designated students participating in arts activities at schools as having increased attainment, cognitive abilities, employability, be twice as likely to volunteer, 20 per cent more likely to vote, and in the case of students from low-income families 'three times more likely to get a degree' (The Cultural Learning Alliance 2011: 1).

The 2015 Report of the Warwick Commission, evaluating the value and future sustainability of culture and creativity in Britain, proposed a key role for cultural institutions as not only lifelong educators and purveyors of leisure experiences, but also as partners within a school, home and 'publicly funded arts and heritage' model of education (Warwick Commission 2015: 15). Cultural settings were posited as instrumental in contributing to a world-class curriculum 'infused with multi-disciplinarity, creativity and enterprise' (ibid.). Cultural placements provide opportunities for critical reflection and analysis of the expectations and aspirations of a focal institution, in relation to the potential societal impact of cultural settings in engaging diverse audiences and participants.

Selecting a cultural placement

ACTIVITY 2

Visit a variety of contrasting cultural institutions and settings, considering in each case:

- What are its aims, primary function, additional roles, provision for key audience?
- How does it fulfil its designated role and engage with audiences and participants?
- Is it publicly, privately or mixed-funded? What impact does this have on its accountability?
- How does it evaluate and disseminate its success e.g. through regular reports? What are its targets or programmes for development?

The term 'cultural institution' is a broad one with potential settings incorporating a diversity of scale, budget, aims and agendas, an essential preliminary in selecting a cultural placement is to review a range of institutions and settings. Ecclesiastical buildings and stately homes incorporate cultural programmes, while the capital's British Museum, Royal Academy and Royal Opera House exemplify eighteenth- and nineteenth-century publicly endowed cultural institutions. Twentieth- and twenty-first century spaces for cultural innovation are frequently sited within industrial settings, such as London's Tate Modern, Liverpool's Tate, Bristol's Arnolfini and Watershed, or in purpose-built sites such as the Warwick Arts Centre combining visual and performance arts. British cultural investment reflects eclectic knowledge and interests with museum collections including historical and contemporary art, ethnography, science, natural and local history, performance venues host a diversity of local, national and international companies, differently abled performers and multi-linguistic productions. British towns and cities often feature a municipal museum, theatre and arts centre, publicly, privately or mixed-funded cultural institutions showcase ground-breaking, challenging or idiosyncratic exhibitions and performances. International conglomerates, such as White Cube Galleries, operate alongside settings such as The Theatre of Small Convenience, a converted Victorian lavatory designated the smallest theatre in the World. Cultural practice also occurs in vernacular settings: community halls, churches and other places of worship, shopping centres, parks, sculpture trails, beaches, woods, gardens, mountains and private houses.

Institutions cater for a broad spectrum of agendas recognising that cultural visits may be motivated by interest in: professional/educational research, specific exhibitions/productions, leisure and tourism. Publicly and privately funded cultural institutions have educational and outreach policies to widen audiences and extend access and participation across groups identified as under-participating. Cultural placements provide mutual benefits for both institutions and students, as well as 'offering developmental opportunities for students ... (and) getting work done', cultural institutions regard placements as 'an integral part of the organisation's graduate recruitment process' (Neugebauer and Evans-Brain 2009: 3). Fanthome (2004: 5) discusses opportunities for students 'to hone the technique of critical reflection' generating 'greater self-knowledge and self-understanding', qualities which can be beneficial to placement settings in supporting ongoing reflective engagement, a core aspect of 'lifelong learning' within contemporary professional practice (ibid.).

Most areas of Britain feature a range of institutions and settings; conurbations close to Bath Spa University offer a wealth of opportunities. As a World Heritage site, Bath hosts 17 museums within the city centre disseminating its Roman, Medieval and Georgian past, approximately six professional theatres, numerous contemporary galleries, informal performance spaces and historic ecclesiastical buildings housing cultural events; Bristol, European Green Capital 2015, houses over 20 museums and contemporary art galleries, approximately a dozen theatres and a diversity of other cultural venues. Such cultural profiles occur in many UK cities, with a corresponding reduction of the sector's capacity dependent not only on population but also area: London leads in cultural provision and participation, while the Midlands score lower in both indices (Arts Council England, 2014).

Cultural placements: benefits and outcomes

ACTIVITY 3

Select a potential cultural placement and consider:

- What outreach and educational programmes take place and how do they extend its aims?

- Does it cater for a range of audiences/participants with different needs and requirements including special needs and disabilities?

- Is there a policy to encourage diverse audiences/participants particularly those currently under-represented?

Cultural institutions respond to and initiate shifts within contemporary culture, stimulating engagement with cultural settings not merely as purveyors of entertainment, but also as potential forces for democratisation, equity and empowerment. The placement will explore the aims and orientation of the setting, its funding bodies, stake-holders, aims and objectives, alongside its educational and outreach strategies. It will provide opportunities to extend understanding and critical thinking in reflecting on provision issues and implementation within a cultural setting, simultaneously developing transferable analytical qualities and skills. While reflection on the setting's key roles and agenda will help expedite the selection process, mutual clarification of objectives is essential in successful implementation.

Targets, shared with the placement setting, may include:

- gaining professional experience to enhance employability within the sector;
- development of transferable skills e.g. management, organisation, public relations, critical reflection;
- researching an aspect of cultural provision;
- addressing learning outcomes within a particular module/programme.

Fanthome described a successful theatre-based cultural placement where volunteer Mutiat assumed responsibility for co-ordinating a community play: acting on her own initiative, problem-solving and gaining insight into 'administration, finance and marketing departments' and understanding 'the importance of teamwork' (Fanthome 2004: 90). Mutiat's enhanced 'self-esteem and sense of achievement' were supported by the 'friendly and stimulating' (p. 91) working environment which fostered her professional confidence and skills. In contrast, volunteer Amelia encountered difficulties on her theatrical placement due to communication issues on both sides. She suggested that 'everyone embarking on a placement should meet their employer before starting work and discuss both the student's expectations and what the organisation can realistically offer' (p. 103); sound advice whether investigating future employment prospects, developing marketable skills, or researching a focal area.

Cultural placements incorporate different timeframes: a short visit of a day or few days; an intensive period of a week or longer; or a day per week over a medium- or long-term period. The following case studies exemplify different timings and cultural institutions.

Cultural placement case studies

The art museum

The Holburne Museum housed in Bath's eighteenth-century Sydney Hotel features Sir Thomas William Holburne's collection, bequeathed to the city in 1882. The collection includes Oriental and European ceramics, paintings, glass, coins, enamels and furniture. The historical galleries were extended, in 2011, by architect Eric Parry's redevelopment of exhibition spaces, café, educational and visitor facilities, and links with Bath's universities were strengthened. Commitment to widening audiences informs its free admission policy (exempting some temporary exhibitions) increasing the Holburne's yearly visitors to 120,000. Funding includes grants and donations, patrons and business sponsorship, University partnerships, commercial income, exhibitions, lectures and concert admissions (The Holburne Museum 2015).

Widening cultural participation is a key Holburne agenda: contemporary artists such as Julian Opie, milliner Stephen Jones and ceramicist Felicity Aylieff engage diverse audiences through exhibitions and educational outreach programmes. Participants include children, young people and adults at all stages of life including retirement; statutory and higher educational institutions; specialists including artists, creative writers and musicians. Community-based projects facilitate cultural engagement, in conjunction with charities targeting mental health, homelessness, and dementia. Staffing in 2014 comprised approximately 20 paid positions with 250 volunteers contributing across all programmes through short-term and on-going placements.

David volunteered weekly for four years at the Holburne Museum; his placement started during his degree, inspired him to apply for PGCE teacher training, and continued throughout the course. The placement was motivated by David's interest in Bath's cultural community and the museum supported him in developing transferable skills: setting up exhibitions; supporting lectures and private views; contributing to the Children's Saturday Club; participating in annual projects linking the Holburne Museum with local educational institutions and artists, such as Big Draw, Light Labyrinth, and Lantern Procession. David appreciated the museum's placement training, which he noted: 'enhanced volunteers' expertise and fostered knowledge-exchange, mutual respect and positive working models'.

A sense of confidence within cultural and educational environments was evident during David's teacher training year where he actively contributed to a short-term museum group placement project with his cohort of PGCE trainees. The project explored both the historical and contemporary collections, in response to the theme Passion for Pattern: Culture and Meaning. The richly patterned and decorative artefacts of the collections, drawn from a wide range of cultural sources provided inspiration for the trainees' print-making and textiles workshops with children on the autistic spectrum, and 'A' level Art students; the collaboratively created banners were exhibited in Holburne Museum's Clore Studio.

David's cultural placement significantly impacted upon his life choices and career. By extending understanding of the processes of cultural and educational institutions, it acted as 'the spark which confirmed a creative educational future'. Head of Learning Christina Parker commented that observing how cultural placement volunteers 'engage with collections, inspires permanent staff to see them afresh'. She noted that it is 'perfect to work with the next generation of teachers who are discovering the potential of the Holburne Museum', a mutual benefit which develops in-service teachers' commitment to forging cultural partnerships within their practice.

The cultural educational charity

The *Ecology of Culture Report* (Holden 2015) examined current literature, practice and perspectives on the extent to which interactions between institutions, practitioners and audiences generate new cultural forms, investigating 'how the arts and creative industries interact and how they influence economic and social wellbeing' (Thomson cited in ibid.: 5). The report identified cultural ecology as 'the complex interdependencies that shape the demand for and production of arts and cultural offerings' (Markussen 2011 cited in Holden 2015: 2), a focus central to the work of cultural educational charity My Future My Choice (MFMC), which initiates interdisciplinary creative heritage projects for young people linking industry with educational and cultural institutions. MFMC aims to raise confidence, self-esteem and aspirations of young people through engagement with arts, science and cultural heritage, inspiring them 'to celebrate and communicate their passion for learning' (My Future My Choice 2015).

Matching AHRC's (Arts and Humanities Research Council) ecological model, MFMC connect: youth groups, theatre companies, radio stations, science parks, and industry with educational and cultural institutions. Partner museums include M Shed and Museum of Bath At Work with their industrial heritage of boats, cranes and bridges; art, history and media at Bristol's Watershed, Arnolfini and City Museum. MFMC projects link arts and sciences, raising participants' awareness of local culture: the arts, environment, aviation, shipwright industries, wartime and transatlantic slave trade history. Project beneficiaries are young people, frequently with limited opportunities, who work with educators, artists, film-makers, engineers and scientists as well as cultural placement volunteers drawn from statutory, higher educational, and industrial sectors. Volunteers share expertise with participants and cultural partners, contributing to creative ideas and enhancing their professional experience, building communication, organisational and leadership skills. Hugh Thomas, MFMC's Director, cited mutual benefits to both participants and volunteers: enrichment of opportunities, insights and aspirations.

MFMC's cross-curricular cultural and creative projects are supported by charitable, educational and industrial grants, and revenue from events and educational resources. MFMC's contribution to Bristol 2015 European Green Capital initiative, *Bristol Loves Tides* (*BLT*), engages young placement volunteers in generating performance, film and presentations on Bristol's tidal patterns to raise awareness of 'the interconnectedness of ecology, biodiversity ... and wilder green spaces of the city' (MFMC 2015). Tim Smit, Founder of Cornwall's Eden Project, advocated *BLT's* capacity to inspire 'a thousand journeys ... fuelled by the greatest gift of all, curiosity' (ibid.). Rondene Vassal, a *BLT* cultural placement volunteer, appreciated the broad range of professional experience MFMC volunteer training provided, to support development of interviewing, broadcasting and presenting techniques. A former Youth Mayor, with career aspirations towards politics and the media, Rondene valued the organisational and journalistic skills gained through the cultural placement with opportunities to hone transferable communication skills supporting volunteers in educating both their peers and the public in sharing *BLT's* environmental message of connectivity and youth empowerment.

Conclusion

Cultural education has been strongly advocated as central to every child's educational heritage, spanning early years to post-eighteen provision, and educationalists suggest incorporating 'visits at each Key Stage to cultural institutions and venues, which might include a museum, a theatre, a gallery, a heritage site, and a cinema' (Sorrell, Roberts and Henley 2014: 116). Warwick Commission promotes cultural partnerships as essential in augmenting the education offered by schools, encouraging active and reflective participation in the arts both for their own sake and to increase engagement across the curriculum, and improve students' economic potential. It challenges cultural deficit as not only socially and economically impoverishing, but also as negatively impacting on indices of cultural diversity and richness, potentially damaging 'our international reputation and trust in the UK as a diverse and tolerant society' (Warwick Commission 2015: 21).

Alongside providing a forum for what is 'pleasurable in life as well as much that is educationally critical and socially essential' (Arts Council England 2014: 4), cultural institutions potentially contribute towards personal empowerment, challenging socio-economic exclusion. Cultural placements therefore provide a key focus for investigating the potential of focal institutions in fulfilling wider educational agendas while addressing their specialist role of cultural provision.

Follow-up activity

- How does the cultural placement communicate and engage with its target community?

- What is its social media presence e.g. website, Facebook profile, Twitter account, and what contribution do they make to its profile?

- How effectively does it communicate the importance of its focal cultural practice?

Further reading

Follow up citations in References for further information and read:

Nicholson, H. (2011) *Theatre, Education and Performance*. Palgrave Macmillan.

Parker, D. (2013) *Creative Partnerships in Practice: Developing Creative Learners*. Bloomsbury Education.

Simon, N. (2010) *The Participatory Museum*. Museum 2.0.

References

Arts Council England (2013a) *Great Art and Culture for Everyone 2010–2020* [online]. Available from: www.artscouncil.org.uk/great-art-and-culture-everyone. [Accessed 21 September 2016].

Arts Council (2013b) *Spend Per Head 2012/13* [online]. Available from: http://webarchive.nationalarchives.gov.uk/20160204101926/http://artscouncil.org.uk/ [Accessed 21 September 2016].

Arts Council England (2014) *The Value of Arts and Culture to People and Society* [online]. Available from: www.artscouncil.org.uk/media/uploads/pdf/The-value-of-arts-and-culture-to-people-and-society-An-evidence-review-TWO.pdf. [Accessed 13 April 2015].

Bourdieu, P. (1989) *Distinction: A Social Critique of the Judgement of Taste*. London: Routledge.

Bourdieu, P. and Darbel, A. (1991) *The Love of Art*. Oxford: Polity Press.

Cultural Learning Alliance (2011) *ImagineNation: The Case For Cultural Learning* [online]. Available from: www.culturallearningalliance.org.uk/userfiles/files/FINAL_ImagineNation_The_Case_for_Cultural_Learning.pdf [Accessed 13 April 2015].

Department for Culture, Media and Sports (DCMS) (2014) *Taking Part 2014/5 Quarter 2 Statistical Release December 2014.* [online]. Available from: www.gov.uk/government/uploads/system/uploads/attachment_data/file/387592/Taking_Part_2014_15_Quarter_2_Report.pdf [Accessed 13 April 2015].

Fanthome, C. (2004) *Work Placements – A Survival Guide for Students.* London: Palgrave Macmillan.

Holden, J. (2015) *The Ecology of Culture.* Swindon: Arts and Humanities Research Council.

My Future My Choice (2015) *My Future My Choice* [online]. Available from: www.myfuturemychoice.co.uk/ [Accessed 13 April 2015].

Neugebauer, J. and Evans-Brain, J. (2009) *Making the Most of Your Placement.* London: Sage.

Oxford Dictionaries. www.oxforddictionaries.com/definition/english/culture.

Sorrell, J., Roberts, P. and Henley, D. (2014) *The Virtuous Circle: Why Creativity and Culture Count.* London: Elliott & Thomson.

The Holburne Museum (2015) The Holbourne Museum [online]. Available from: www.holburne.org/ [Accessed 13 April 2015].

Warwick Commission (2015) *Enriching Britain: Culture, Creativity and Growth: the 2015 Report by the Warwick Commission on the Future of Cultural Value* [online]. Available from: www2.warwick.ac.uk/research/warwickcommission/futureculture/finalreport/enriching_britain_-_culture_creativity_and_growth.pdf [Accessed 13 April 2015].

Williams, R. (1958) 'Culture Is Ordinary'. In Higgins, J. ed. (2001) *The Raymond Williams Reader.* Oxford: Blackwell.

8

Learning on field trips and study visits

Disrupting assumptions through listening, observation and reflection

Lone Hattingh

Purpose of the chapter

This chapter will enable you to develop your understanding and reflect on:

■ the importance of socio-cultural perspectives in early childhood theory and practice;

■ factors influencing understandings of a range of perspectives such as the child's position in society and the role of the adults working with children;

■ the ways in which students are able to explore and challenge their own perspectives when confronted by unfamiliar and challenging contexts.

Introduction

This chapter reports and reflects on a week-long field trip to Denmark, undertaken by a group of 15 students in their final year of a BA Honours degree in Early Childhood from Bath Spa University. While some students were studying full time, intending to train as teachers on completing their Bachelor degree, others were employed in Early Years settings alongside their university studies. The field trip was arranged as a supplement to final year degree modules, with the purpose of enriching and broadening students' knowledge and understanding of approaches to early childhood education. Gilbert *et al.* (2013) suggest that students develop deeply reflective thinking, and are able to consider and apply different perspectives in their own professional development as a result of the transformative nature of experiential learning on residential field trips. An initial aim of the field trip was to enable the student participants to challenge their own assumptions about early childhood education, and to consider their experiences in the light of cultural and social contexts which were unfamiliar to them. Dahlberg and Moss (2005: 63) call for a 'recognition of multiple discourses which encourage dialogue and reflection'.

Practical considerations of the field trip were taken into account in arranging and coordinating visits to a range of settings in Copenhagen with the aim of providing a window onto early schooling, nursery and forest experiences within a Nordic context. Students visited each setting for a full day where possible; they did this in groups of between three and six, and stayed in these groups throughout the week. This provided each student with a partner with whom they could share ideas and reflections, while helping each other to find their way around the city. One day was set aside for a university visit in Copenhagen, where students were given the opportunity to meet and have lunch with other students, and to attend a lecture.

This chapter begins by considering the participating students' reflections. This is followed by a discussion of the relevance of these reflections in relation to theoretical insights and perspectives. Finally, some suggestions for reflection and further reading are provided.

Throughout this chapter, adults working with children in the settings are referred to as 'teachers'.

ACTIVITY 1

Reflect on your own practice, and how you might incorporate a new or different perspective into your work with children. Where might you look to find sources of inspiration?

Reflections on shared experiences

Each evening, students gathered in the hotel as a whole group, to discuss their different experiences and to reflect on their meanings in relation to their existing knowledge and understanding, and their practice. Gilbert *et al.* (2013) conclude that students are able to reflect on experiential learning opportunities both individually and through shared understandings brought about by participation in group residential field trips. In this way, students' reflections, meanings and perspectives are shared and negotiated through dialogue and discussion. The choice of location for the field trip was influenced by the understanding that the Nordic countries are considered to provide early childhood care and education which views children both as individuals, and as participants in wider society (Woodrow and Press 2008). This perception is reflected in Danish societal culture, with its emphasis on the child as a citizen (Dahlberg *et al.* 2007). Hedegaard (2014) calls for an awareness of culturally sensitive approaches to early childhood education, rather than immersing everyday practice in an unquestioning acceptance of taken-for-granted assumptions, which are influenced by an adherence to 'traditional' child development theories. This awareness was made visible by one student's comments:

> Above all, I feel so much more aware of the way culture influences behaviour and I have really been questioning myself a lot more, and why we do what we do rather than accepting the things I am used to.

A particular point of interest was that practitioners in the preschool settings encouraged children to develop and follow their own interests in a way that reflected a sense of trust in children's competence. Dahlberg and Moss (2005) describe prevailing attitudes to early childhood education as being dominated by expectations on children to fit in with the adults' perspectives, into a world which is dominated by a need to learn technical skills as they prepare for school. This stands in contrast to a view of early years settings as 'sites for ethical and political practice' (Dahlberg and Moss 2005: 11), where children are encouraged to explore possibilities in their quest to develop their own perspectives and understandings.

> The ... pedagogy displays a sense of trust in children being agents of their own learning. It really opened my eyes to the way men are much more involved in working with children ... these settings made huge impressions on me and my thoughts on early years practice.
>
> (Student 1)

Perspectives on equality were foregrounded by observations of male practitioners working closely with children in the settings they visited, something only occasionally seen by the students in their home settings. The role of men was very noticeable, and their nurturing role was visible particularly with the very young children in the nurseries.

The openness and willingness of teachers to develop dialogues with the children helped to create a context where children's everyday learning experiences were valued and encouraged. This resonates with Fleer's (2010) contention that it is the immediacy and reality of children's play that is important. One student remarked that 'the one clear point (that stood out) was to take a small step back and let the children become a lot more independent and take more risks'. Another commented that the relationships which were nurtured between teachers, and between teachers and children, provided a meaningful context for shared dialogue and meaning. The way in which children were encouraged to follow and develop their own interests created an environment in which teachers were responsive to children's interests in their playful endeavours.

'This opened my eyes to the impact free flow play can have on children as young as they were. Also the relationships between staff members and children were highly inspiring and motivating' (Student 2).

During a visit to a forest setting in the deer forest near Copenhagen, teachers were enthusiastic in explaining underlying theoretical principles of their approach, making explicit links between theory and their own practice. The setting clearly encouraged the adults to consider themselves as practitioner-researchers, and to firmly locate their practice within theoretical frames.

Any international trip is a fantastic way to adapt our practice and learn from other cultures' education systems. Speaking to staff about their education system allowed me to gain a deeper understanding, allowing me to make connections.

Allowing children to take risks as part of their developing understanding about their world and themselves as competent learners, was particularly evident in visits to the forest experience settings. Students found that both adults and children were accepting of cold and wet weather (the field trip was undertaken in December), and understood the need to consider each other, and to take responsibility for their own actions.

> The day we had in the forest school was completely eye opening. … The way the adults were with the children, the energy, the atmosphere was absolutely wonderful. I was really interested in how 'outside' everything was. No one complained about being cold, no one cried when they fell over.
>
> (Student 1)

Students commented that the issue of health and safety was visibly different to that in the England. They were struck by the sense of trust encouraged between children and adults, with children in school being able to move around freely. One student was particularly inspired by the view of the child as a citizen: someone who had ideas and perspectives of their own. In the primary school, children were seen to take responsibility for the crossing outside the school, and to present ideas at whole school assembly while calling on their fellow students to become involved in groups working for common interests, such as the environment. Dahlberg *et al.* (2007) suggest that children have the knowledge and power to take their own place in society; the adults were pursuing dialogic relationships with them, where children's views were seen as important and powerful.

A number of students remarked on the way in which they had been empowered to examine their own practice in their settings. One commented that, after returning home to her work setting, she had shared her experiences on the field trip with her colleagues: 'the impact and reflections on my practice has been quite interesting. On returning I discussed with my colleagues what I had learnt and experienced'. Another reported that 'since the trip I have carried out a presentation within my workplace and highlighted the differences in practice from perspectives (gained on the field trip)'. As a team we discussed these differences and reflected on our own practice. I was keen to highlight the differences in the view of the child and the trust that was very apparent in every setting we visited as well as the trust in the practitioners.

Students reflected on the funding provided for childcare in Denmark, and the affordability for parents as a result. School starting age of six years was noted, as was the custom of babies sleeping outside and the value placed on outdoor pursuits in general:

> I hope that in the future you will be able to offer other students the same opportunity as I really feel it was so beneficial; not only to my work at university, but professionally as a future teacher and on a more personal level. With regard to my practice, I have really reflected on the underlying trust that the adults have of the children, and although this may too be culturally relative, I wonder how this could be instilled in English settings?

ACTIVITY 2

Reflect on an aspect of your way of working with young children, which might warrant a fresh and new perspective. How could you challenge your own beliefs and understanding in order to empower children to become more active agents of their own learning and doing?

Discussion

The students' responses reflected an engagement with the child's competence and position in society. Meanings were interpreted by focusing on the child both as an individual person and as a participant and member of a group (for example: the family, the educational setting) and wider society (Hedegaard 2010). This perspective of interpersonal experiences which are embedded in social contexts, underpins Vygotsky's contention that 'socially rooted and historically developed activities' lead to intrapersonal transformation (1978: 57). Vygotsky (1978) suggests that, rather than children learning along a horizontal developmental path, their learning takes place through a range of experiences which are woven together, particularly during play. Play, and in particular pretend or role play, creates a zone of proximal development for the child, where he 'behaves beyond his average age …; in play, it is as though he were a head taller that himself' (Vygotsky 1978: 102). Vygotskian theory underpins a cultural–historical frame within which to locate the students' reflections and responses. An important aspect of cultural–historical theory is that children's learning takes place in the social context: it is shaped by societal experiences which are rooted in the culture of institutional environments of the family, home and the educational setting.

Also influential in cultural–historical theory is Rogoff's well known research on culture and development. Rogoff (2003: 237) stands alongside Vygotsky in her emphasis on the value of the social context for learning, defining socio-cultural theory as an 'integrated approach to human development' where 'individual cognitive skills are derived from people's engagement in socio-cultural activities'. The integrated approach to learning and development resonates with Hedegaard (2012) and Fleer's (2011) holistic theoretical lens, which avoids separating the elements of learning by acknowledging the interrelatedness of all aspects of the social context.

The students' experiences and observations of free play and the relationships which were fostered in the settings, reflected an acknowledgement of the child's learning and development in cultural and social contexts. Stetsenko and Ho (2015: 223) describe it thus: close observations of play can prompt discussions into 'what makes us human, how we are positioned in the world, and what our world is all about'. They go on to suggest that 'play provides context for children to forge their own voices' while 'co-authoring meaning with others', and highlights the reciprocal nature of individuality and social interaction (Stetsenko and Ho 2015: 232). In their analysis of cultural–historical approaches, both Fleer (2011) and Hedegaard (2012) call for a 'wholeness approach', where the child's relationship with the cultural environment and social situation is seen as an important element of their learning and development. This approach provides a lens through which to view children's experiences, and challenges traditional maturational theories of play and learning which are associated with predominantly Western, developmental understandings. It avoids seeing children's experiences as separate elements, and instead takes account of the socio-cultural context within which they find themselves. The planning of visits to settings on the field trip, which enabled small groups of students to spend extended periods of each day in different institutions, provided them with a window onto a cultural–historical approach which recognises the importance of learning through play and experience in relation to the context and environment as a whole.

Fleer (2011) carried out research to explore the ways in which kindergarten teachers could frame children's learning, play and development within cultural–historical theory while endeavouring to meet required outcomes of policy and curriculum without compromise. Fleer's research focuses on the traditionally held belief that young children learn through play, and her findings demonstrate that children are capable of using their imaginations to develop complex concepts within a playful socio-cultural context, supported by a pedagogy which is founded on strong theoretical principles.

Underlying the students' observations while visiting settings, was the interaction between teachers and children. Relationships were seen as 'motivating', with children and adults playing and working together, although children were also given time and space to develop their ideas and their thinking without interruption. This allows for the child's perspective to be valued and acknowledged. Sommer *et al.* (2010; 2013) propose five assumptions behind a child-perspective approach: amongst these is the 'dialogic process between the child and the … teacher, where both contribute to the learning objective'. In this way, children are regarded as equals even though they have less life experience and knowledge; the child's perspective and point of view is valued. Sommer *et al.* (2010; 2013) argue that, while the adult needs to provide care and support, it is the child's perspective – 'the sense they make of things – that has to be accepted and used as a platform for giving children new challenges and opportunities'.

A cultural–historical approach (Fleer 2011; Hedegaard 2012) facilitates a child perspective approach by acknowledging the dialogic nature of relationships in the setting, and by valuing the role that is played by the cultural and social context. This acknowledges the role of the child as an individual, as well as an active member of society.

Conclusion

In considering the impact of the field trip, students noticed a different focus in early childhood education where it appeared that children's social skills and independence was valued above cognitive skills in the early years. It was challenging and interesting to interpret the children's meanings as students relied on body language, tone and context when in settings as, although the adults spoke fluent English, the children conversed in Danish. This might have resulted in some of the children's conversations being missed or misinterpreted. The forest experiences were particularly valued by the students. Children 'just got on with things', 'ate food that was given to them', and spent a great deal of time outdoors 'regardless of the weather'. Cultural differences were very noticeable, and not necessarily what had been expected. The experience encouraged a critically reflective approach, which recognised the value of reflection in challenging the students' own established and taken-for-granted assumptions. Different theoretical frames and concepts of childhood were made visible by means of dialogue, observation, experience and reflection.

Further reading

Dahlberg, G., Moss, P. and Pence, A. (2007) *Beyond Quality in Early Childhood Education and Care: Postmodern Perspectives*. London: RoutledgeFalmer.

Hedegaard, M., Fleer, M., Bang, J. and Hviid, P. (2010) *Studying Children: A Cultural–Historical Approach*. Maidenhead: Open University Press.

Rogoff, B. (2003) *The Cultural Nature of Human Development*. Oxford: Oxford University Press.

References

Dahlberg, G. and Moss, P. (2005) *Ethics and Politics in Early Childhood Education*. London: RoutledgeFalmer.

Dahlberg, G., Moss, P. and Pence, A. (2007) *Beyond Quality in Early Childhood Education and Care: Postmodern Perspectives*. 2nd edn. London: RoutledgeFalmer.

Fleer, M. (2006) 'The Cultural Construction of Child Development: Creating Institutional and Cultural Intersubjectivity'. *International Journal of Early Years Education* 14 (2): 127–140.

Fleer, M. (2010) *Early Learning and Development: Cultural–Historical Concepts in Play*. Cambridge: Cambridge University Press.

Fleer, M. (2011) 'Kindergartens in Cognitive Times: Imagination as a Dialectical Relation between Play and Learning'. *International Journal of Early Childhood* 43 (2): 245–259.

Gilbert, L., Rose, J., Palmer, S. and Fuller, M. (2013) 'Active Engagement, Emotional Impact and Changes in Practice Arising from a Residential Field Trip'. *International Journal of Early Years Education* 21(1): 22–38.

Hedegaard, M. (2010) 'A Cultural–Historical Theory of Children's Development'. In Hedegaard, M., Fleer, M., Bang, J. and Hviid, P. eds *Studying Children: A Cultural–Historical Approach.* Maidenhead: Open University Press: 10–29.

Hedegaard, M. (2012) 'The Dynamic Aspects in Children's Learning and Development'. In Hedegaard, M., Edwards, A. and Fleer, M. eds *Motives in Children's Development: Cultural–Historical Approaches.* Cambridge: Cambridge University Press: 9–27.

Hedegaard, M. (2014) 'The Significance of Demands and Motives Across Practices in Children's Learning and Development: An Analysis of Learning in Home and in School'. *Learning, Culture and Social Interaction* 3 (2): 188–194.

Rogoff, B. (2003) *The Cultural Nature of Human Development.* Oxford: Oxford University Press.

Sommer, D., Pramling Samuelsson, I. and Hundeide, K. (2010) *Child Perspectives and Children's Perspectives in Theory and Practice.* London: Springer.

Sommer, D., Pramling Samuelsson, I. and Hundeide, K. (2013) 'Early Childhood Care and Education: A Child Perspective Paradigm'. *European Early Childhood Education Research Journal* 21 (4): 459–475.

Stetsenko, A. and Ho, P.G.C. (2015) 'The Serious Joy and the Joyful Work of Play: Children Becoming Agentive Actors in Co-Authoring Themselves and Their World Through Their Play'. *International Journal of Early Childhood* 47 (2): 221–234.

Vygotsky, L.S. (1978) *Mind in Society.* London, Harvard University Press.

Woodrow, C. and Press, F. (2008) '(Re)Positioning the Child in the Policy/Politics of Early Childhood'. In Farquhar, S. and Fitzsimons, P. eds *Philosophy of Early Childhood Education: Transforming Narratives.* Oxford: Blackwell Publishing: 88–101.

9

Working with students with specific learning difficulties/ dyslexia on placement

Mary Dooley

Purpose of the chapter

After reading this chapter you should understand:

- what is meant by SpLD/dyslexia and how dyslexia is defined and understood;

- the challenges faced by and competencies of dyslexic learners in the classroom;

- the professional challenges and opportunities for the teacher;

- career options with a focus on supporting SpLD/dyslexia learners.

Introduction

When I was a newly qualified teacher I was lucky enough to be offered a job in a special school working with young people who had wide ranging additional educational needs. This wonderful experience started me on a long and fulfilling career within education. Working with all children is an enriching experience, but in my view working with children and adults who have additional needs is particularly gratifying. I am quite old now (55 as I write this chapter), and my journey through work has taken me from special schools, to mainstream inclusive educational settings; from early years to higher education. As I progressed on the journey, I chose to specialise within the field of SpLD/dyslexia. In return to my showing enthusiasm and commitment to additional needs, inclusion and equality; the most exciting learning experiences came to me. Hopefully this is a journey you also want to undertake and will find this chapter useful.

I am sure that the first question in your mind is what is dyslexia? And what on earth is SpLD?

SpLD is the acronym for specific learning difficulty, and dyslexia is one form of SpLD. SpLD is an umbrella term that is sometimes incorrectly used as a synonym for dyslexia. However dyslexia is one form of SpLD, others include dyscalculia, dysgraphia, dyspraxia and attention deficit (hyperactivity) disorder. Some agencies such as the SpLD/Dyslexia Trust and the Professional Association for Teachers and Assessors of Students with Specific Learning Difficulties (PATOSS) prefer to use the umbrella term SpLD alongside the term dyslexia.

An individual with dyslexia has an educational profile that exhibits a difficulty that 'primarily affects the skills involved in accurate and fluent word reading and spelling'(Rose 2009). However dyslexic learners have complex and individual learning profiles and there are 'no clear cut off points' (Rose 2009) as to where a learner is identified as having one form of SpLD such as dyslexia and another such as dyspraxia.

So if that all sounds fairly vague I am afraid that defining dyslexia is also viewed as problematic (Elliott and Grigorenko 2014). There is no universally agreed definition of dyslexia, however within England we can look to some key authoritative voices to give us an overview of currently widely accepted definitions.

The British Psychological Society (BPS 1999) definition links to reading/spelling accuracy and fluency and describes:

> Dyslexia is evident when accurate and fluent word reading and/or spelling develops very incompletely or with great difficulty. This focuses on literacy at the word level and implies that the problem is severe and persistent despite appropriate learning opportunities.

However more recent definitions tend to be broader and recognise complex learning needs that extend beyond reading and spelling. In his independent report to the secretary of state for children, schools and families (2009), Sir Jim Rose defined dyslexia as:

- Dyslexia is a learning difficulty that primarily affects the skills involved in accurate and fluent word reading and spelling.

- Characteristic features of dyslexia are difficulties in phonological awareness, verbal memory and verbal processing speed.

- Dyslexia occurs across the range of intellectual abilities. It is best thought of as a continuum, not a distinct category, and there are no clear cut-off points.

- Co-occurring difficulties may be seen in aspects of language, motor co-ordination, mental calculation, concentration and personal organisation, but these are not, by themselves, markers of dyslexia.

- A good indication of the severity and persistence of dyslexic difficulties can be gained by examining how the individual responds or has responded to well-founded intervention.

This description was adopted by the British Dyslexia Association (BDA) Management Board, but with the addition of the further paragraph shown below,

> In addition to these characteristics, the BDA acknowledges the visual and auditory processing difficulties that some individuals with dyslexia can experience, and points out that dyslexic readers can show a combination of abilities and difficulties that affect the learning process. Some also have strengths in other areas, such as design, problem solving, creative skills, interactive skills and oral skills.
>
> (Peer 2006)

As you will see from the above, definitions evolve and build on previous understanding. Likewise as practitioners we need to keep ourselves up to date with current research and discussion about SpLD/dyslexia, there are many 'myths' that surround people's understanding of dyslexia (Elliott and Grigorenko 2014) and whilst on placement a common experience of students is to find some of these 'myths' perpetuated. Credible sources of information such as the British Dyslexia Association or the SpLD Trust provide us with a useful overview of an evolving understanding of dyslexia. Perhaps the most important thing to recognise is that whilst the BDA states that dyslexia 'mainly affects the development of literacy and language related skills', it is best thought of as a continuum (Rose 2009) or dimension (Hulme and Snowling 2009). This continuum of dyslexia not only encompasses learning differences related to literacy that will range from mild to severe, but also learning differences that are comorbid with other forms of SpLD. Hulme and Snowling (2009) describe comorbidity as the co-occurrence of two different disorders or diseases in the same individual. Within the context of SpLD/dyslexia, it is increasingly being recognised that dyslexia frequently occurs alongside other learning differences, and that the neurological basis for these conditions may have a great deal of commonality. In their study of the relationship between ADHD and dyslexia, McGrath *et al.* (2011) have found that whilst reading disabilities may affect approximately 5 per cent of the population, there is a likelihood that between 25 per cent and 40 per cent of children with one disorder will also meet the criteria for the other. Because dyslexia is a continuum of need and also frequently co-occurring with other disabilities, whilst on your placement you may find it useful to think of children as having a range of highly individual needs that may have features of dyslexia as well as other learning differences, to a greater or lesser extent. Supporting wide ranging additional needs is the responsibility of all staff and *The Teacher's Standards* (2013) make it clear that it is every teacher's responsibility to 'have a clear understanding of the needs of all pupils, including those with special educational needs … and be able to use and evaluate distinctive teaching approaches to engage and support them' (DfE 2013: 12).

This brings me to another really important point. Whilst on placement you will discover that every person with dyslexia will exhibit a unique learning profile, and will have a different story to tell you. So make sure you see the individual before you assume the needs that may be attached to a specific learning label.

ACTIVITY 1

Reflect on your answers to the following questions:

■   What experience do you have of SpLD/dyslexia in the classroom?

■   In view of issues such as comorbidity, what are your views on the usefulness of using labels such as dyslexia?

■   What might you consider the challenges and opportunities for teachers in mainstream classrooms?

What can you learn from the dyslexic learner?

The educational system in England has a strong emphasis on being highly literate as a primary means to success. In most subjects being able to work rapidly and fluently with text is often an essential expectation. However many learners (not just those with dyslexia/SpLD) may find it extremely demanding to achieve the required levels of competence. Through your observation and discussion whilst on placement, you will see that many learners have developed highly effective strategies in order to be able to cope. Dr Lindsay Peer (2006) describes how 'some learners have very well developed creative skills and/or interpersonal skills, others have strong oral skills. Some have no outstanding talents. All have strengths'. It is often through their strengths that learners with SpLD/dyslexia develop strategies to succeed. The strengths that you may observe include skills in areas such as:

■   teamwork;

■   speaking and listening;

■   visual and spatial skills;

■   metacognition;

■   creative approaches to problem solving;

■   maximising the use of technology;

■   perseverance;

■   individualised strategies.

Once you start to notice these strengths you move away from a deficit based view of individuals with learning differences, to an affirmative model as described by Swain and French:

It is essentially a non-tragic view of disability and impairment which encompasses positive social identities, both individual and collective, for disabled people grounded in the benefits of lifestyle and life experiences of being impaired and disabled.

(2003: 150)

The affirmative view of dyslexia recognises the potential richness of a world that values other skills alongside competence in literacy. Many of these skills are extremely important throughout life. Many adults with dyslexia become highly successful despite the problems that they might have faced (and continue to face) with literacy and learning (Logan 2009). For those of you who are thinking of careers within education you can begin to tailor pupil support to maximise strengths. This is not just good teaching for the dyslexic learner, but good teaching for all:

> Special educational provision is underpinned by high quality teaching and is compromised by anything less.
>
> (DfE 2015: 25)

Sadly some individuals with dyslexia will also have become demotivated by the difficulties they can experience within education systems (Dahle *et al.* 2011), and on placement you may also observe people who cope through very negative feelings or behaviours. In these incidences it is important to look past the behaviour and see if you can identify whether there are unmet additional learning needs. Current educational policy asks for strategies with 'a focus on inclusive practice and removing barriers to learning' (DfE 2015: 20). For all pupils, including those who are demotivated, educational settings are being expected to adjust their methods in order to ensure that the curriculum is accessible to all. Through the Children and Families Act (HM Government 2014, pt 3: 20) the law now identifies that a child or young person has a learning difficulty, including dyslexia, if they have: 'a significantly greater difficulty in learning than the majority of others of the same age'. The Special Educational Needs and Disability Act (HM Government 2001) states that an education provider has a duty to make 'reasonable adjustments' to ensure disabled students are not discriminated against. Using your placement time to observe and talk to both the individuals with dyslexia and the staff, will help you to gain an understanding of what adjustments can be made. I am the course tutor for a module entitled 'Professional practice: Supporting the dyslexia learner in the classroom'. Many of the students who attend this course opt to undertake a placement within an educational setting. The placements provide a wealth of learning opportunities, and on return our students frequently comment on how varied and creative placements are in removing barriers for learners with dyslexia to enable them to have full access to the curriculum.

Case study

Michelle undertook her placement within a primary school in Bristol. She was very impressed with the commitment to meeting the needs of all pupils and described the support the school were offering one mildly dyslexic pupil she observed. The new SENCO had targeted staff training in SpLD/dyslexia, and where previously informal identification of dyslexia had be undertaken by one member of the support staff, there was now an extensive training programme for all staff with more than ten teaching staff trained to identify pupils with dyslexia. The school had a strong supportive ethos for pupils with additional needs, and this was evident amongst both staff and pupils. Michelle described how she felt teachers went 'above and beyond' to support children with difficulties such as dyslexia. The school had considered the classroom learning environment, the teaching and the curriculum, and had made adaptations to support the children with SpLD/dyslexia. The pupil's dyslexia particularly affected his spelling, and visual perception. The school had given the pupil coloured overlays to use for reading and a book with blue paper in with which to write. On the wall were commonly confused phonemes/words with visual images to act as a prompt, for example, a picture of a bed to support pupils who got b's and d's confused. Throughout the school, pastel coloured paper was used in preference to white, and dyslexia friendly larger fonts had been selected for use to aid pupils with the visual perception issues sometimes associated with dyslexia.

ACTIVITY 2

In the light of what you have learned so far consider the steps you may wish to take in order to prepare for a placement where learners with SpLD/dyslexia will be present. What preliminary actions might you take (e.g. speaking with the classroom teacher and/or the SENCO; accessing school policies on inclusion and special needs; familiarising yourself with key resources and the academic literature concerning SpLD).

Guidance on how to make the most of your placement

With this chapter in mind, I asked a group of students what key points they would pass on to others interested in undertaking placements. This is a summary of their advice.

Observe and support

Whilst on placement you can feel pressured to be actively supporting throughout the day, however, this is one of the times of your life when you may have the opportunity to step back and observe. Observe the learners (as individuals and in groups), the educators and the learning environment. But be very careful not to make children or young people with learning differences feel singled out from their peers. Studies such as those done by Burden (2005) reported that academic self concept for children with dyslexia is lower than for those without. Developing an awareness of the importance of your role in helping to boost confidence is extremely important. In a YouGov survey (Dyslexia Action 2012: 18) more than 57 per cent of parents felt their child had a negative experience at school because of their dyslexia and 37 per cent reported staff as making unhelpful comments like 'try harder', which then had a negative impact on self-esteem. You may need to work on the basis of whole class, rather than individual support, unless you feel confident that pupils won't feel stigmatised.

Learn from the learners

The people who can tell you the most about their learning differences are the pupils themselves.

Talk to all the learners including those with the learning difference. You don't need to draw attention to a deficit. Focus on their strengths 'I like the way you.' 'Can you tell me how you … ?' 'What do you think about … ?' 'What is your experience of … ?'

They are the experts about their own learning, and are often very pleased to be acknowledged as such. Many people feel empowered through greater discussion and self-advocacy regarding their learning needs.

Collaborate

Teamwork is core to most jobs, and essential when working in an educational setting. On placement you become a member of the professional team. Try to enhance your understanding of additional needs by asking to meet the full range of team members, from those who give individual student-based support, to those responsible for special educational needs (SEN) organisation and policy. Engage with all setting staff to discuss learning difference. Make use of the wealth of expertise you will find. Many settings will have staff with higher level qualifications linked to SEN, talk to them to find out their journeys, their pedagogy, their strategies and approaches.

Within most settings there are files relating to learners with additional needs. Many of these will be confidential, but with appropriate permissions it can be very useful for you to access some of this information.

At all times you should be working under the guidance of the professional with responsibility for SEN within the setting, and you need to ensure you feedback relevant information to them.

Develop support strategies

There are many excellent texts that suggest context specific strategies to support the dyslexic learner. Most support similar principles regarding effective teaching strategies. A survey of practitioners who were consulted for the Rose review (2009) identified the following as features of good practice when working with dyslexic learners:

- using multisensory methods for teaching and encouraging multisensory learning;
- planning and delivering lessons so that pupils/students experience success;

- planning and adapting the teaching programme to meet individual needs;
- teaching a structured programme of phonics;
- building in regular opportunities for consolidation and reinforcement of teaching points already covered;
- maintaining rapport with pupils/students;
- planning a purposeful and engaging balance of activities in lessons;
- teaching pupils/students to be aware of their own learning strategies;
- teaching pupils/students to develop effective learning strategies;
- showing sensitivity to the emotional needs of pupils/students;
- teaching pupils/students to improve their working memory;
- selecting appropriate resources to support particular learning needs.

(Dyslexia Action 2012: 31)

This guidance can be adapted to fit your role within the placement and to meet the requirements of the individuals you encounter.

ACTIVITY 3

At the end of your placement it is good practice to reflect on what you have learned.
Return to the questions in Activity 1 of this chapter.

- How has your experience challenged your assumptions about working with SpLD/dyslexic learners?
- How has your understanding of the role of professionals within education been shaped by your conversations with learners with SpLD/dyslexia?
- What might be your next steps in developing your understanding and experiences/competencies in this area?

The journey ahead

If, like me, you love your time working with people with learning differences, you may wish to look for training opportunities to further enhance your skills.

A good starting point is the websites of the British Dyslexia Association (BDA), Dyslexia Action, the Professional Association for Teachers and Assessors of Students with Specific Learning Difficulties (PATOSS) and the SpLD/Dyslexia Trust. They offer guidance regarding a range of training courses and accredited programmes for education staff working with learners who have SpLD/dyslexia. These courses are delivered in a number of ways including open learning courses, onsite training, and e-learning.

Your local university, further education college and the Open University are all likely to offer further training opportunities. Further experience can be gained by volunteering within schools and other educational organisations.

There are plenty of employment opportunities within SpLD/dyslexia such as:

- specialist teaching assistant/learning support assistants;
- educational publishing and resources;
- private dyslexia tutors;
- SEN learning aids and software companies;
- specialist SEN teachers;
- special educational needs coordinators;
- educational psychologists;
- dyslexia trainers;
- occupational therapy;
- speech and language therapy;
- dyslexia assessors.

There is an increasing recognition of the needs of dyslexic learners. From Key Stage One, where schools are required to undertake structured phonics programmes in accordance with the recommendations from the Rose Review; to initial teacher education where courses are required to incorporate teaching training regarding the needs of pupils with dyslexia.

Taking advantage of the opportunity of an educational placement is often an important first step in discovering what interests you and where your talents lie. You will recognise that people learn in very different ways. Dyslexic learners benefit from multi-sensory techniques, which build on their strengths and the range of strategies they may already employ. Methods that engage learners with SpLD/dyslexia are the same methods that engage all learners. Over the years I have changed my thinking, I have moved away from seeing learning disabilities, to understanding learning differences. All learners employ different learning methods within different learning situations, there is no one size fits all for education. We are all learners.

References

Burden, R. (2005) *Dyslexia and Self-Concept*. London: Whurr.

British Psychological Society (1999) *Dyslexia, Literacy and Psychological Assessment*. Leicester: British Psychological Society.

Dahle A.E., Knivsberg, A. and Andreassen, A. (2011) 'Coexisting Problem Behaviour in Severe Dyslexia'. *British Journal of Research in Special Educational Needs* 11 (3): 162–170.

Department for Education (DfE) (2013) *The Teachers' Standards*. London: Department for Education.

Available from www.gov.uk/government/uploads/system/uploads/attachment_data/file/301107/Teachers__Standards.pdf.

Department for Education (DfE) (2015) *Special Educational Needs and Disability Code of Practice: 0–25 years*. London: Department for Education. Available from www.gov.uk/government/uploads/system/uploads/attachment_data/file/398815/SEND_Code_of_Practice_January_2015.pdf.

Dyslexia Action (2012) *Dyslexia Still Matters*. Surrey: Dyslexia Action. Available from www.dyslexiaaction.org.uk/files/dyslexiaaction/dyslexia_still_matters.pdf.

Elliott, J. and Grigorenko, E.L. (2014) *The Dyslexia Debate*. New York: Cambridge University Press.

HM Government (2001) *The Special Educational Needs and Disability Act*. London: The Stationery Office. Available from www.legislation.gov.uk/ukpga/2001/10/contents.

HM Government (2014) *Children and Families Act*. London: The Stationery Office. Available from www.legislation.gov.uk/ukpga/2014/6/pdfs/ukpga_20140006_en.pdf part 3; 20).

Hulme, C. and Snowling, M.J. (2009) *Developmental Disorders of Language Learning and Cognition*. Oxford: Wiley–Blackwell.

Logan, J. (2009) 'Dyslexic Entrepreneurs: The Incidence, Their Coping Strategies and Their Business Skills'. *Dyslexia* 15 (3): 328–346.

McGrath, L.M., Pennington, B.P., Shanaham, M.A., Santerre-Lemmon, L.E., Barnard, H.D. and Willcutt, E.G. (2011) 'A Multiple Deficit Model of Reading Disability and Attention-Deficit/Hyperactivity Disorder: Searching for Shared Cognitive Deficits'. *Journal of Child Psychology and Psychiatry* 52: 547–557.

Miles, T. (1991) 'On Determining the Prevalence of Dyslexia'. In Snowling, M.J. and Thomson, M.E. eds *Dyslexia: Integrating Theory and Practice*. Wiley: Chichester: 144–153.

Rose, J. (2009) *Identifying and Teaching Children and Young People with Dyslexia and Literacy Difficulties (The Rose Report)*. Nottingham: DCSF Publications.

Peer, L. (2006) *Code of Practice for Employers*: British Dyslexia Association. Available from www.bdadyslexia.org.uk/dyslexic/definitions.

Swain, J. and French, S. (2003) 'Towards an Affirmation Model of Disability'. In Nind, M., Rix, J., Sheehy, K. and Simmons, K. eds *Inclusive Education: Diverse Perspectives*, London: David Fulton: 150–164.

10

International placements

Dan Davies

Purpose of the chapter

After reading this chapter you should understand:

- rationales for international placements in higher education within a broader framework of internationalisation;

- the potential for international placements to both challenge and reinforce students' cultural stereotypes;

- some of the ways in which international placements can enhance learning in both comparative education and personal vocation;

- the importance of careful planning and cultural induction to maximise benefits from such experiences.

Introduction

'Internationalisation' is a buzz-word in current UK higher education discourse, by which universities can mean a number of related activities. At one level it may imply simply the recruitment of more international students to offset shortfalls in other kinds of income, but it can also include curriculum changes to draw upon more international contexts or theories for study. A significant component of internationalisation for most universities is 'outward mobility'; providing opportunities for students to study or work overseas for varying periods. Degree courses in modern foreign languages have traditionally included a year abroad as part of a four-year structure, whilst under the European Union-funded Erasmus programme, students from all subject disciplines have had the opportunity to spend a semester of their programme studying in an EU partner institution. For a variety of reasons – both financial and language-related – the uptake of Erasmus funding by UK-based students has lagged behind their counterparts in other EU countries, so universities have increasingly sought shorter-term opportunities for greater numbers of their students to have some international experience as part of their studies.

The rationale for providing such opportunities tends towards a variation on the old adage 'travel broadens the mind'. A notion of globalisation is often invoked, within which students can be more effectively prepared for lives and careers in a world where international borders become increasingly irrelevant. The development of intercultural understanding is also significant here; an experience in which students live and work with people in a different cultural context is likely to lead to deeper learning than a tourist visit to the same place. The resulting empathy may be transferred back into the multicultural context within which students live and study in the UK, though outward mobility is often seen as more important for those in regional universities, who may not be exposed to such diversity in their home institution. In relation to student placements or visits to countries in the 'Global South' or 'Majority World' (sometimes pejoratively referred to as the 'Developing World'), the development of intercultural understanding is sharpened into challenging student stereotypes of such countries, thus contributing to their awareness of global citizenship, social justice and development issues.

ACTIVITY 1

Why do you want to go on an international placement? Make a list of the factors that motivate you to gain international experience. Here are some suggestions:

- to gain intercultural understanding or raise your awareness of a culture different from your own;
- to improve your professional or employability skills;
- to gain new global perspectives on your own life or society;
- to see new parts of the world, but not as a tourist.

Be honest with yourself and list *all* the reasons you'd like to go, even the seemingly trivial (e.g. 'have fun', 'get a suntan') to try and understand your underlying rationale for applying. Think about other ways in which you might fulfil some of these aspirations that might be less demanding (e.g. going on holiday or applying for a volunteer programme). You may want to make a list of pros and cons of undertaking an international placement, which may well be quite stressful, costly or isolating, to be sure that it's really what you want to do. This process will also be helpful to you in completing any application forms.

There is indeed evidence that Western university students hold a range of stereotypical images of Majority World countries. Shaw and Wainryb (1999: 469) found a widespread perception of homogeneity concerning the beliefs and practices of individuals in 'other' cultures, a view that 'excludes analyses of the dynamics of societies, including the many struggles, conflicts and disagreements among people in asymmetrical relations of power' and 'oversimplifies aspects of what appear to be multifaceted and often conflict ridden, cultural and psychological realities'. Brown (2006) argues that an emphasis on poverty in student beliefs creates the perception that the sole remedy is through charitable donation, a view that reiterates the neocolonial stereotype of the 'South' as needy and passive. Challenging such beliefs within a university programme is difficult where there is physical and cultural separation, students have limited life experiences and educators have limited resources. Thus, 'felt knowledge', which may materialise during study visits, makes development issues immediate to the learner and 'address(es) some of the problems spawned by the relational nature of development education' (McRae 1990: 113). Several education departments in UK universities have established links with various types of educational institution (schools, colleges, universities) in the Majority World, some of which include student placements. One such is the link between the BA Education Studies programme at Bath Spa University and Mufulira College of Education in the Copperbelt region of Zambia.

The Bath Spa – Mufulira placement

The relationship between Bath Spa University and Mufulira College of Education was established in 2004, building on a British Council-funded link between clusters of schools in the localities of the respective institutions. Participating Bath Spa students are drawn from a second year undergraduate module entitled 'Education and International Development', which examines generic educational and development issues through case studies in different African countries. The module provides a strong historical, social, political and economic context for the study of education in Africa; Finney and Orr (1995) stress that conveying information and providing cross-cultural experiences will be ineffective without political and social contextualisation to change prejudices and misunderstandings. Participating students – who are mainly self-funding though some travel bursaries are available – are paired with primary trainee teachers at Mufulira College and spend three weeks learning alongside their Zambian colleagues for a day per week in a teacher training programme. They spend four days per week observing pedagogy in three types of primary school (government, private and community). Whilst in schools, students are given guidance on aspects of pedagogy and curriculum to focus their study. Students' observations and analysis of the wider issues raised by this visit are written up as a report and submitted as part of the formal assessment for the module. The twelfth group of between 10 and 19 students visited Mufulira in May–June 2015; bringing the total number of participants to 137 since the inception of the link. Although several members of staff from Mufulira College have been funded to visit the UK, to date no Zambian students have been able to participate in a reciprocal placement.

ACTIVITY 2

What international placements or experiences are available to you through your course, department, faculty or university? If you're studying at a university within the European Union it is likely that you will be able to apply for an Erasmus Student Mobility grant, which will enable you to study for a semester (usually around six months) at a partner university elsewhere in the EU. Language skills, or the willingness to learn a new language in a short time, are often required for Erasmus placements, though an increasing number of European universities offer courses in English. There may be opportunities for shorter-term placements that you can apply for, such as the Zambia experience described above, or self-directed placements as part of an international placement module. Try to find out from the staff organising such placements as much as you can about what is on offer. How long is it? What are participants expected to do whilst there? Do you need to organise your own travel and/or accommodation or is this done centrally? What vaccinations will be required? Are travel bursaries available or is the trip self-funded? How much is it likely to cost (including core and optional activities)? What requirements are there for written, oral or other reports on the visit and are these assessed?

Student learning from international placements

Although the majority of participants in the Bath Spa – Mufulira visit describe the experience as 'life-changing' on their return, we need to exercise caution in claiming transformational learning from such placements. Kambutu and Nganga (2007) report on student teacher learning from a cultural immersion programme in Kenya, for which the participants completed pre- and post-visit surveys. While the data revealed gains in awareness, understanding and appreciation of the host culture, aspects of ethnocentricity remained. The students' initial preconceptions of life in Kenya centred around apprehension, education and lack of modern amenities. Although their post-visit reflections evidenced some change in perceptions of Kenya, participants revealed other degrees of ethnocentrism as they referred to their own cultural practices as the only point of reference. In order to strengthen visit participants' understanding of postcolonial influences and to help them reflect upon their beliefs, Martin (2008) argues for a stronger critical literacy framework linking North–South. Andreotti and Warwick (2007: 1) describe critical literacy as a way of helping students analyse 'relationships amongst language, power, social practices, identities and inequalities, to imagine "otherwise", to engage ethically with difference and to understand the potential implications of their thoughts and actions'. It is based on the assumption that knowledge is partial, incomplete and constructed according to one's context and experiences, and as a result, it is imperative to engage with one's own perspectives as well as other perspectives to transform views, identities and relationships. This process of reflection on assumptions and reconciling them with present experiences may cause discomfort, but the value of 'unfinishedness' should result in more open-minded and dynamic beliefs. However, the entire premise that simple exposure to different cultures can dismantle stereotypes and build stronger understanding of development has been challenged (Lee 2006). Hutchings and Smart (2007) caution that some study visits to countries of the South continue to reinforce stereotypes and inequalities.

In order to answer the question 'in what ways does first-hand experience of a developing country's education system challenge British students' preconceptions and help them to understand development issues?', I conducted a small-scale study of the Bath Spa–Mufulira placement (Davies and Lam 2010). Initially, all participants completed a short questionnaire concerning their beliefs about Africa and African education at the beginning and end of the module. These provided the background data with which to compare the insights evidenced in the written reports of those who had visited Zambia. Following initial analysis of these written reports, three students were selected for interview by a colleague on the basis of their different responses to the experience. 'Simon' was the only male participant in the placement. He is white and was brought up in a middle-class family in a medium-sized city in the South West of England. Lynn was a second year education student with an Iranian ethnic heritage, who was brought up in a middle-class neighbourhood on the outskirts of London. Tracy is white and comes from a middle-class family in a medium-sized city in the South of England. At the time of the interview, all three were considering their career options, including the possibility of teacher training.

'Simon'

Simon's preconceptions about Africa at the beginning of the module were of poverty, suffering and over-population; he mentioned political instability in Zimbabwe, ethnic cleansing in Darfur and riots over elections in Kenya, whilst recognising that these images were strongly influenced by media coverage at the time. Simon's motivation to travel to Zambia was to see for himself whether the images he had of 'unhappy' people were 'true'; a desire strengthened by the insights he gained during the taught module: 'I found that after gaining a brief theoretical understanding of these countries, I wanted to develop a deeper understanding by gaining a first-hand experience.' He realised that Zambian society and history were more complex than he had been expecting – he hadn't realised that before the 1970s oil crisis and copper price crash it had been considered a 'middle income' country – and that national statistics can disguise huge regional and local variations. This complex view had changed his expectations of what he would experience visiting other countries in the region:

> I would expect to find a lot of community spirit; large groups of people who know each other, support each other. Really friendly people ... inequality as well; rich people living side by side with poor people.

Although Simon was conscious of not replacing his notions of poverty with a 'poor but happy' stereotype, he was struck by the disparities of wealth he observed and was particularly challenged by the private school he visited. He was surprised by the level of resourcing and small class sizes in a country with such a low GDP per capita. The experience of community cohesion despite inequalities led Simon to reflect upon his own life in the UK and recognise some of the deficits in contemporary British society.

As a committed future primary school teacher, Simon felt that the experience in different learning and teaching environments would help to inform and develop his own practice. He was struck by 'how much you can achieve with so few resources'. Although appreciative of the educational technology available in English primary schools, Simon was able to make the links between his practice and that which he observed, talking about how learning objectives could be planned for and achieved with 'only a blackboard and piece of chalk'. His observations appeared to reinforce his own transmission pedagogy – he referred to the 'imparting of knowledge' as the core of education. However, the requirement to plan and teach lessons in the Zambian schools was for him the most significant learning experience of the visit, and one he contrasted most strongly with the theoretical learning he had gained from the module. Overall, the visit had led him to reflect upon his own teaching, which he claimed would be henceforth less reliant on technology and resources, whilst focusing on what he saw as the 'basics' of sound pedagogy.

Simon's experience of going to Zambia further enforced his commitment to education and interest in the country. The added value of actually visiting Zambia, for Simon, was in the beginning to see the history and policy outlined in the module lecture (given by the Principal of the College, visiting the UK at the time) from multiple Zambian perspectives, by immersing himself in the culture:

> This was quite a genuine, authentic experience. The knowledge we gained (from the placement) was so much deeper, and is reflected in the way we can now talk about our experiences. If we attempted to talk about it after the lecture we would have some idea, but we can now give a fuller, deeper account of the system and how it works.

He participated wholeheartedly in the placement, taking every opportunity to observe lessons, read government documents and talk with lecturers, teachers, students and pupils in rural Zambia. He was a strong advocate for the experience on his return; one of two students who volunteered to talk to the following year's cohort, urging them to participate in this 'life changing' experience.

'Lynn'

Before participating in the placement, Lynn did not distinguish between individual African countries:

[I] viewed the whole of Africa – I know it's a continent with lots of countries – but all being the same with each country excluding South Africa, all very poverty stricken.

Lynn recalled her initial images of Zambia as a: 'very deprived country, raggedy clothes, high risk of AIDS'. Tracy had images of Africa before the module consisting of 'happy children' with very few resources, which she claimed had come from media coverage. Lynn also reported her initial thoughts about 'education borrowing' (Steiner-Khamsi 2004) for the purpose of improving education:

> I didn't understand before I went why they hadn't looked at Europe and seen this is the way we need to do it … This is a pretty narrow minded point of view and I didn't understand about the money issues.

Whilst acknowledging the limitations of this viewpoint, Lynn appeared to have retained a naïve perspective on educational borrowing even after the placement, being apparently unaware of the strong British colonial influence on Zambian education:

> We've been getting it right, not right, but there's been a way of doing it all around the world, everyone else seems to have managed to do it … I don't understand why they hadn't observed us more and invested more time in their education system.

For Lynn, the experience of visiting Zambia helped to reinforce the content presented in the Education in Africa module, but also made it much more immediate and personal: 'seeing it in reality is completely different and really wakes you up and helps you come to terms with the reality of it'. It is clear that from Lynn's perspective, the experience of visiting Zambia was well complemented by content exposure to the African context through the module. For example, the diversity of the module also helped her to understand the differences between countries in the African continent:

> We just went to Zambia, so if I hadn't learnt about the other countries and done the comparative studies in class, I would have just one view of what I thought the whole of Africa would have been like, which isn't the case because each country's so different. It sort of broadened my expectations.

Lynn appeared to have had some of her preconceptions challenged by the placement; for example she was surprised to see such a large private sector in the education system. She also acknowledged that visiting Zambia had revealed aspects of nationalism, patriotism and a strong sense of community. Lynn identified a contradiction within her impressions of Zambia with regards to money, as in her view there did not appear to be a middle class – either individuals had money or were in poverty, with little middle ground.

Lynn emphasised the skills she had gained from the placement, such as 'interpersonal skills … learning how to teach without a classroom full of resources, how to improvise with what you had opposed to relying on materials'. Like Simon, she was able to relate classroom observations in Zambia to her own learning as a future professional:

> I learnt a lot from other teachers, how they control a class of 80 children, different techniques used, group work, asking each other for help rather than going to teacher, won't have time to go to every child. … Learning to work with a variety of children with all age ranges and abilities. You might have a 14 year old and an 8 year old in the same class, having to amend the way you talk to different people.

While these observations have helped Lynn to relate her experience to education in England, there appears to be an emphasis on how much Zambian teachers are able to accomplish whilst lacking resources, rather than any reference to the innate benefits of their teaching methods for pupil–teacher relationships and group cohesion. This perhaps relates to her neo-colonial attitudes towards education in Africa expressed above. However, Lynn also noted how her experience of overcoming language barriers in Zambia could inform her practice in multilingual contexts in the UK: 'you'll have a lot of kids who won't have strong English, learning to overcome that and give them the same education as everyone else'.

Lynn also credited the placement with confirming her vocation as a teacher, based on her experience in the community schools where teachers are unpaid and, in Lynn's view, passionate about education:

> They're in there every day benefiting the community and the country. That is such an important thing that I've taken away, knowing that this is definitely what I want to do, knowing that I'm going to make a difference, and hopefully I'll be as passionate and willing as those people in the community school.

Although Lynn was able to reflect on her experiences of education in Zambia and the skills gained through the placement, some of her naïve preconceptions of the African continent had only been modified to an extent. When asked how she would approach other African countries, Lynn admitted that: 'it sounds bad, but I would probably relate them in my mind as being pretty similar still'. Whilst acknowledging that different countries would be likely to experience different issues, she still saw Africa as profoundly 'other': 'I wouldn't compare it to the West or anything'. She was also critical of education reforms in Africa, and struggled to understand why polices had taken so long to be introduced and implemented. This may be due to a lack of awareness of the complexities surrounding education reform, the way in which aid has been targeted, the constraints imposed by a debt burden and the role of local and international initiatives.

'Tracy'

Tracy found it difficult to articulate both her preconceptions and postconceptions, and how they changed as a result of the placement. She found some of her impressions problematic and confusing, particularly pertaining to poverty. On the one hand, she felt that the poverty was not as 'bad' as imagined, but on the other hand, the impact of seeing it was 'a lot worse because you don't put a face to it'. The visual impact of the images of poverty struck Tracy, as she noted: 'I think you don't really understand it till you see it, I think you can learn all the statistics, everything you want, but you won't get a picture of it until you see it.' However, she was apparently surprised to see school buildings, where she had perhaps expected outdoor classrooms under the shade of a tree. Tracy recounted one episode in which children asked for more gifts after the visiting students presented a school with some resources, and the teacher proceeded to carry out an activity in which children were asked to name what they would like the students to bring for their next visit to Zambia. When asked to describe her reaction to this incident, Tracy admitted that:

> We were horrified. We thought it was quite wrong to get the children's hopes up. We want to help but we haven't got a lot of money ourselves. We expected them to be pleased with what we've given them.

Yet when asked if this incident challenged the image of 'happy children', Tracy supported this image of the children, and attempts to explain their reaction:

> (E)ven when they're asking they're still happy, it was just the teaching staff who made it a sort of game. They were still happy and smiley; it was only the really poor children who were begging for food. They seemed to be happy with what they'd got 'til it was pointed out to them that they could ask for more.

For Tracy, her visits to schools appear to have been full of contradictions. For example, she was surprised that some of the private schools did not have as many text books as state schools. Although there were computers at the private schools, frequent power failures reduced the usefulness of this resource. This led her to question why parents were willing to pay for a private education with few resources and smaller classrooms than the government schools, though she recognised the value of having smaller numbers of children in each class.

Tracy's experience of seeing the lived experiences of teaching in government schools was shocking: 'the teacher I was with wasn't qualified, so she'd grab a few text books and she'd say, "have you learnt about this?"'. However, Tracy made it clear that the opportunity to go to Zambia exposed her to a different culture and showed her aspects of another education system. In particular, she was inspired by the teachers in the community school who volunteered their time to help others 'have a better future'.

When asked about incidents from the trip that challenged her preconceptions, Tracy had difficulty responding and her interview responses indicated a struggle to understand what she learned from the experience of going to Zambia. Yet she was able to articulate the apparent simplicity of outlook she observed in the Zambians she met, which seemed to have a profound impact on the way in which she viewed her choices in life: 'There's something we could learn, our way of life is so complicated, so stressful.' It is clear that this statement is complicated, or perhaps even contradicted with the example she mentions of a wedding of a young girl, which made her reflect on the amount of choice in England and the degree to which human rights are enjoyed:

> You respect what you've got more and I hope that doesn't go away. You learn about how other people live, and although poverty is horrible for the people living in it, they make the most of what they've got and are probably happier than a lot of people in the West.

Despite this inner conflict and inability to express the tension of conceptions and experiences, the trip affected Tracy profoundly, and enabled her to reconsider her current life choices. She explains:

> I was having trouble with my boyfriend at uni; we live together and I wasn't sure it was working. Going out there made me realise there's so much to life; if you're not happy with something just move on. We take so much for granted, we should just use what we've got and enjoy life as much as we can because some people don't have much choice.

Tracy's stereotype of 'happy children' in Africa appears to have been reinforced by the placement, as she described the inspiration she had gained from the welcoming nature and eagerness of the Zambians: 'Lots of things inspired me, the way everyone's so welcoming, they've got nothing but they want to give you what they've got. I've never known so many people to be so friendly.' Tracy also expressed cohesion between her learning and interest in Zambia. She noted that the placement had definitely added value to the university-based learning: 'especially at this level, you're given so much information so quickly, it's hard to distinguish, but when you actually experience it, you never forget that … '. Zambia and Zambians became very important to Tracy personally, as evidenced in her heightened interest in the country:

> I actually care more about it, because it's not just figures thrown at me, you actually see how it is and take an interest in it, now if anything comes up about Zambia, I'll read up on it and be really interested in what it has to say.

Overall, the international placement experience had several benefits for Simon, Lynn and Tracy as individuals, and led to different kinds of learning from those associated with the university-based module of which the visit was a part. In particular, there is some evidence of gains in awareness, understanding and appreciation of Zambian culture, as found by Kambutu and Nganga (2007). However, their responses also revealed a number of limitations of the visit, including the persistence or even reinforcement of ethnocentric stereotypes (Finney and Orr 1995) and a tendency to over-simplify complex issues of inequality (Shaw and Wainryb 1999). Evidence from previous studies (e.g. Andreotti and Warwick 2007; Burr 2008; Martin 2008) suggests that in order to remedy some of these deficiencies, two substantive changes are required to the programme. The first of these is to include a stronger critical literacy dimension to the preparation for the visit, to provide students with a framework informed by post-colonial theory through which to make sense of their experiences.

ACTIVITY 3

Once you have chosen your placement, how can you best prepare yourself? It goes without saying that you'll need to find out as much as you can about the country you're visiting from websites and guide-books. Find out about the climate and likely weather conditions at the time of year you'll be visiting, together with cultural expectations of dress, to enable you to pack accordingly. If you will be working in schools, nurseries, colleges or universities try to find out as much as you can about the country's education system (for example numbers of years of compulsory primary and secondary schooling, balance of public and private provision, length of the school day, average class sizes, structure of any national or regional curricula). Try to learn a few words of the local language, such as 'hello', 'please', 'thank you' and 'goodbye' as this will be much appreciated and helps to break down any initial barriers. Try to get to know any fellow placement participants, so you can work together well when you get there and plan jointly for any teaching or other activities you may be expected to lead.

Tips for successful international placement experience

The tips below relate closely to the questions above and draw upon the experience of successive cohorts of students participating in the Zambian placement forming the basis for this chapter:

- Be as clear as possible in your own mind why you want to go on the placement and what you hope to get out of it.

- Prepare thoroughly: find out as much as you can about the country and its people, the region/city/town/village(s) you'll be placed in and the context for the educational setting where you will work.

- Pack carefully but travel light: most placement organisers will provide a 'kit list' so ensure you bring all the essentials but try to be ruthless with optional extras that 'might come in handy' as the extra weight will be a burden and could limit the things you'll bring home with you.

- Take some small, light presents for hosts: photographs of you, your family and home town are often appreciated. In some countries, photos of popular members of the British Royal Family also go down well!

- Be sensitive to cultural expectations. Some cultures are more formal than those you may have experienced previously, so be guided by your hosts in manners of greeting and particularly styles of dress. Bare shoulders, short skirts or trousers worn in public can sometimes offend.

- Be flexible in your expectations of what will happen and when. Communication issues, cultural expectations and infrastructure difficulties can all lead to unexpected changes in your programme. Just relax, 'go with the flow' and be open to whatever new experiences your international placement offers you.

- Make the most of every opportunity to engage with the local community. Don't put yourself at risk but respond warmly if you have opportunities to share meals or stay with nationals of the country you're visiting. You will learn more and have a richer experience by sometimes stepping outside your 'comfort zone'.

The suggestions above may seem obvious, but it is sometimes easy to forget the original reasons you chose to undertake an international placement when you're feeling homesick or everything seems unfamiliar and alien. You won't enjoy all aspects of your overseas experience, however, it is important to reflect on experiences of discomfort to analyse any underlying stereotypes or unrealistic expectations you may have which are preventing you from getting the most out of it. If you're clear about your motivation for going, are well-prepared and open to really participating in a different cultural context it can be a truly life changing experience!

Further reading

McKeown, J. (2009) *The First Time Effect: The Impact of Study Abroad on College Student Intellectual Development*. Albany: State University of New York Press.

Midwinter, D. and Whatmore, T. (2011) *Positive Placements: Making the Most of Your Educational Placement*. London: Continuum.

Van Mol, C. (2014) *Intra-European Student Mobility in International Higher Education Circuits*. Houndmills: Palgrave Macmillan.

References

Andreotti, V. and Warwick, P. (2007) Engaging Students with Controversial Issues Through a Dialogue Based Approach. *CitizED*. www.citized.info/?strand=0&r_menu=res.

Brown, K. (2006) School Linking and Teaching and Learning Global Citizenship. *CitizED*. www.citized.info/pdf/commarticles/Kate_Brown.pdf.

Burr, M. (2008) *Thinking about Linking?* DEA Thinkpiece. http://think-global.org.uk/resource/thinking-about-linking/

Davies, D. and Lam, E. (2010) 'The Role of First-hand Experience in the Development Education of University Students'. *International Journal of Development Education and Global Learning* 2 (2): 35–52.

Finney, S. and Orr, J. (1995) 'I've Really Learned a Lot, but … ': Cross-cultural Understanding and Teacher Education in a Racist Society'. *Journal of Teacher Education* 46 (5): 327–333.

Hutchings, M. and Smart, S. (2007) *Evaluation of the Impact on UK Schools of the VSO/NAHT Pilot Scheme: 'International Extended Placements for School Leaders'.* Unpublished report, Institute for Policy Studies in Education, London Metropolitan University.

Kambutu, J. and Nganga, L.W. (2007) 'In These Uncertain Times: Educators Build Cultural Awareness Through Planned International Experiences'. *Teaching and Teacher Education* 24 (4): 939–951.

Lee, M.M. (2006) '"Going Global": Conceptualization of the "Other" and Interpretation of Cross-cultural Experience in an All-White, Rural Learning Environment'. *Ethnography and Education* 1 (2): 197–213.

Martin, F. (2008) 'Mutual Learning: the Impact of a Study Visit Course on UK Teachers' Knowledge and Understanding of Global Partnerships'. *Critical Literacy: Theories and Practices* 2 (1): 60–75.

McRae, L. (1990) 'Development Education: Theory and Practice'. Doctoral Thesis. Toronto: Ontario Institute for Studies in Education, University of Toronto.

Shaw, L. and Wainryb, C. (1999) 'The Outsider's Perspective: Young Adults' Judgments on Social Practices of Other Cultures'. *British Journal of Developmental Psychology* 17 (3): 451–471.

Steiner-Khamsi (2004) *The Global Politics of Educational Borrowing and Lending.* New York: Teachers College Press.

11

Youth and community work placements

Laura Green

Purpose of the chapter

This chapter provides students with an understanding of:

- key historical and political developments that have shaped youth and community work in the UK;

- the variety of spaces, settings and circumstances within which youth work operates;

- core values and methods that typify youth work practice;

- the value and impact of youth and community work placements for students.

The changing context of youth work in the UK

The history of youth work in the UK is complex and contradictory. Lacking a definitive policy home of its own, youth work has always existed in a policy environment that appears resolute to shift, squeeze and restructure the profession in diverging and contradictory ways (Bright 2015). Youth work was founded by a mixture of philanthropic, social action and Christian voluntary organisations with agendas to 'do good' and provide young people with social, emotional, political and spiritual support. It was in 1939 that these activities became formally institutionalised in policy, The Service of Youth (Board of Education 1939) set out an intention to offer activities for young people that sought to enhance leisure-time learning. Little further work to organise youth services took place until after World War Two, and a subsequent 'sense of post-war mutuality embodied the state's commitment to public services' (Bradford 2015: 26) served as the catalyst for the formation of a committee chaired by Countess Albermarle to report on how youth services might support young people in times of 'changing social and industrial conditions' (Ministry of Education 1960: 1). The Albermarle Report recommended the expansion and professionalisation of youth services predicated upon the identification and management of the problem of youth through: 'association, train-ing and challenge of the right kind' (Ministry of Education 1960: 52). The report heralded a 'golden age' for youth work and the following 20 years saw significant expenditure for rapid expansion in services to youth, training initiatives for the workforce and a growth in the for-mally developed body of professional knowledge underpinning the profession. The arrival of Thatcherism and the New Right brought a re-politicising of welfare policy, a drive towards individual responsibility and a weakening of support for collectivised provision (Bradford 2012). Reassigned as a non-essential service, in contrast to social work, criminal justice, schools and further education, seen as higher priorities, youth services took the brunt of cuts to funding and therefore services. The trend was undisrupted by the coming to power of New Labour in 1997, which introduced what it termed Third Way politics, which sought to trouble previous political and ideological dualisms: 'capital versus labour, conservative versus radical, left versus right, state versus the individual' (Sercombe 2015: 43). However, in essence, for youth work what transpired was a re-envisioning of neoliberal approaches introduced by the previous Conservative government. Since then, like other public services, for example schools and hospitals, youth work has become increasingly subjected to quasi-market meas-ures of accountability, there are pressures to work only with those deemed most 'at risk' or 'in need'. Youth workers are expected to quantify the impact they make on the lives of young people through an emphasis on recorded outcomes (which demonstrate acquisition of a 'soft skill' for example increased confidence), and accredited outcomes (a standardised outcome which is externally validated, for example, GCSEs or Duke of Edinburgh Awards), and youth services became accountable to Ofsted (Tyler 2009).

While in the past youth work has taken place in dedicated spaces and predominantly within statutory youth and/or social services, today youth workers can be found within broader multi-agency teams and partnerships with differing and often conflicting agendas. Cuts to services, and competition for funding of youth activities has led to an increased focus on targeted support for particular groups of young people such as Looked After Children (LAC), young parents, young offenders and young carers. In addition, there is often a require-ment for youth workers to evidence their contribution to policy agendas in local authorities such as the reduction in NEETs (young people identified as not in employment, education and training), crime prevention, health initiatives, and employability (Wood, Westwood and Thompson 2015). These conditions have far reaching effects on the nature of the work that can be delivered and many youth workers struggle with the tension between such conditions and efforts to maintain the core values of youth work. Therefore it is vital that students under-taking placements in youth and community work settings be aware of the principles that underpin youth work approaches and how they may contribute to this, often within contexts that make fidelity to this approach challenging.

Core values of youth and community work practice

To understand the nature of any profession it is useful to consider the National Occupational Standards that guide it, in relation to youth work the overall identified goal is:

> To enable young people to develop holistically, working with them to facilitate their personal, social and educational development, to enable them to develop their voice, influence and place in society and to reach their full potential.
>
> (Lifelong Learning UK 2008)

Youth and community work represents a vastly diverse and shifting professional field, youth workers can be found not only in youth clubs but in places such as schools, colleges, Youth Offending Teams, hospitals, careers guidance services, drug projects to name only a few. Approaches and methods of youth and community work differ greatly according to context and application, leading critics to argue that such diversification has led to an inevitable 'watering down' of the true nature of the work (Jeffs and Smith 2010). In opposition to this, other youth work scholars argue the benefits of occupying liminal space and multi-purpose roles in young people's lives, describing youth workers as 'the last of the great generalists' (Ingram and Harris 2013: 72). They argue that it is this generalist approach that is of benefit to the work; since the absence of a fixed and constrictive curriculum, typical of other educational systems such as schools, enables youth work to 'begin where the young people are, not from where we would like them to be' (ibid.).

In understanding the role of a youth worker it is useful to explore ethical and professional principles set out for youth workers within the National Youth Agency (NYA) Statement of Ethical Conduct in Youth Work.

The National Youth Agency Statement of Ethical Conduct in Youth Work

Ethical principles

Youth workers have a commitment to:

1   Treat young people with respect, valuing each individual and avoiding negative discrimination.

2   Respect and promote young people's rights to make their own decisions and choices, unless the welfare or legitimate interests of themselves or others are seriously threatened.

3   Promote and ensure the welfare and safety of young people, while permitting them to learn through undertaking challenging educational activities.

4   Contribute towards the promotion of social justice for young people and in society generally, through encouraging respect for difference and diversity and challenging discrimination.

Professional principles

Youth workers have a commitment to:

5   Recognise the boundaries between personal and professional life and be aware of the need to balance a caring and supportive relationship with young people with appropriate professional distance.

6   Recognise the need to be accountable to young people, their parents or guardians, colleagues, funders, wider society and others with relevant interest in the work, and that these accountabilities may be in conflict.

7   Develop and maintain the required skills and competence to do the job.

8   Work for conditions in employing agencies where these principles are discussed, evaluated and upheld.

(National Youth Agency 2004: 6)

It can be observed by this code that there is an acknowledgement of diversity within the field of youth work, and therefore a consequent lack of specific and prescriptive guidance for ethical and professional practice. This emphasises the importance of applying professional judgement in making ethical and professional decisions. Despite this diversity there remains a core set of values and principles, methods and approaches that can be said to define work undertaken in this field: voluntarism and universalism, association and informal education, and anti-oppressive practice (National Youth Agency 2004).

Voluntarism and universalism

The principle of voluntarism distinguishes youth work from virtually all other services targeted at this age group (typically 12 to 24 years of age). Unlike schools, traditionally young people have chosen to freely engage in youth work activities, and have entered into (and disengaged from) youth work relationships by their own choice. This has a particular impact on the ways in which relationships between young people and youth work practitioners are developed and maintained. The likelihood of young people choosing to access a youth provision is conditional on their perception of whether they feel that provision acknowledges and addresses their needs and desires. Young people choose to take part in youth work projects, usually during their leisure time, and as such they retain the power to 'vote with their feet' should they find that projects hold no attraction in terms of activities or working practices. The value of voluntarism therefore reasserts a commitment by youth workers to centralise young people's experiences as the starting point for practice.

Universalism in youth work has traditionally meant that services are open access and therefore any young person or group of young people are free to participate. This is another unique aspect of the youth work approach, since it means that youth workers will tend to work with, rather than in spite of, or even against, existing peer groups. Youth workers value young people's affiliations and friendships and build upon these to develop meaningful, genuine and sustainable opportunities for shared learning experiences.

Shifts in policy and cuts to generic youth service funding have inevitably resulted in a reduction of the universal service available to young people. A justification for this has been the need to target work at those 'most in need', moving the spotlight from early intervention and equality of access to 'crisis intervention'. The rising focus on 'targeted support' means that often projects are funded and developed exclusively with particular groups in mind, for example Looked After Children, therefore working against the goal of offering universal provision. Many practitioners attempt to mitigate against this by ensuring that part of their provision is offered as open access, or by developing opportunities for wider community engagement as part of their planned programme, however, this still results in the diminishing of universal work. Targeting provision to 'at-risk' groups has also meant an increase in the number of young people that are referred by other agencies to youth provisions sometimes (for example as a result of stipulations of an Anti Social Behaviour Order or a Youth Conditional Caution) compulsorily. This constraint on young people's choice to engage presents a challenge to youth workers because it is seen in direct opposition to voluntarism, however, practitioners in such settings attempt to retain this value by conceptualising voluntarism 'not simply as an absence of compulsion, but the pursuit of the young person's willingness to take part' (Payne 2009: 224). It can be observed that even in voluntary settings, some young people choose not to positively engage with youth workers, while, in compulsory provision young people will often respond enthusiastically to youth workers they feel respect and care for them, and so:

> What is significant about the ideal of voluntarism is that youth work can only proceed effectively if the young people choose to participate and if they take some responsibility for the relational elements of the youth work process.

> (Ingram and Harris 2013: 74)

In their search for space to value voluntarism youth workers draw on the importance of respectful, reciprocal relationships with young people as fundamental to their work, this will be discussed in greater depth later in this chapter.

ACTIVITY 1

List all of the groups and organisations you attended as a young person. Did you attend voluntarily or compulsorily? How did this shape your expectations of your role and the role of adults? How did this shape your expectations for involvement?

Association and informal education

The principle of association may be defined as the 'development of community and learning through shared life and experience' (Bright 2015: 2) and characterised by the coming together of people, in camaraderie, to explore issues and skills around social, emotional and political aspects of their lives. This principle is underpinned and reinforced by the values we have just explored: voluntarism and universalism; as well as by the use of group work and informal education as predominant pedagogical methods in youth work (op. cit.).

Informal education, developed over many years through practice in community and youth work settings, now provides a significant body of knowledge, theory and critique that guides and influences work far beyond that which takes place in youth and community centres. It is not possible in such a short chapter to develop in-depth theoretical explanations of informal education, however, in the context of this book on education placements, it is important to make a distinction between the approaches to learning utilised in youth work and other more formal settings.

Despite their multifarious role in young people's lives, youth workers are primarily educators. They engage with young people in diverse settings with a view to developing opportunities for informal learning. This means, starting where the young people are rather than beginning projects with prearranged aims and objectives. The goals are to provide dynamic experiences that facilitate personal and social development:

> Youth workers purposefully intervene in young people's lives, creating opportunities, activities and conversations that aim to enable young people to think, feel and act differently towards their social world.
>
> (Wood, Westwood and Thompson 2015: 2)

Essential to this informal approach is the use of purposeful conversation and dialogue (Batsleer 2008) as a process of collective critical enquiry. Conversation between young people and youth workers lies at the heart of good youth work (Batsleer 2008; Jeffs and Smith 1996; Young 1999). All planned activities, trips, projects and events can be regarded as a stimulus for the development of opportunities for learning conversations. Conversation is founded within supportive, helping relationships and it is important that this should be seen as part of, rather than in isolation to, the deliberative and proactive nature of the work. Informal learning is led by the concerns and interests of the learner, recognises diverse starting points, abilities and motivations and, importantly, values the process of learning above a predetermined end result or qualification. As such, youth workers understandably struggle with the remit set by New Labour and successive governments to evidence young people's learning (and in turn the effectiveness of youth work practice) through the achievement of formally acknowledged accreditations such as Duke of Edinburgh Awards and ASDAN (Award Scheme Development and Accreditation Network) qualifications. Smith (2008,

TABLE 11.1 A continuum of informal and formal education (adapted from Smith 2008)

Informal Conversation based	Negotiated curriculum	Formal Set curriculum

Table 11.1) proposes that developing a dichotomy between formal and informal education is unhelpful and suggests that viewing these on a continuum, with informal education at one end of the scale, and formal education at the other, and including an area that emphasises a 'negotiated curriculum' in the centre, provides a tool for better positioning differing approaches to practice.

This continuum acts as a useful means for exploring the debates within youth work, surrounding the incorporation of more formal methods of monitoring, and provides scope for developing opportunities for informal learning within the constraints of formal settings. Essential to processes of informal education are working practices that are underpinned by social justice, valuing of personal experience and anti-oppressive practice.

Anti-oppressive practice

A core principle of youth and community work is the deliberate intention to address discrimination and oppression by actively challenging inequality and working for social justice, not only in provision but in wider society (National Youth Agency 2004). It is important to distinguish between anti-discriminatory practice, which is a requirement to operate within society's legal framework; and anti-oppressive practice, defined as 'understanding oppression and power, commitment to empowerment and the ability to reflect, critically analyse and change practice' (Chouhan 2009: 61). This positions youth workers dynamically as actors of social change, as opposed to practitioners simply concerned with avoiding unlawful discrimination. As a result, reflective practitioners are required to examine their own attitudes, values and privileges, reflexivity requires the worker to consider how the social values they hold structure their responses to particular people and circumstances. Lena Dominelli outlines the essential nature of self-reflection for practitioners:

> Challenging inequality and transforming social relations is an integral part of anti-oppressive practice. Knowing oneself better equips an individual for undertaking this task. Self-knowledge is a central component of the repertoire of skills held by a reflective practitioner ... Moreover, reflexivity and social change form the bedrock upon which anti-oppressive practitioners build their interventions.
>
> (Dominelli 2002: 9)

ACTIVITY 2

1   Make a list of all the aspects of your identity that you think might shape the way you view the world.

2   Consider how these factors might impact on the way you view others or their life choices.

3   Are there any types of people that you would find it difficult to work with? Why?

Youth workers attempt to challenge the assumptions of others, including young people; question grand narratives or universal truths predicated upon deeply embedded structures; and consider alternatives (ibid.). Youth workers will necessarily consider social divisions that relate to status and power in society, such as gender, ethnicity, sexuality, class, age and dis/ability, and where these intersect and will concern themselves with 'the "network" of social relationships, institutions and groupings – which play an important role in the distribution of power, status and opportunity' (Thompson 2006: 21).

Thompson's (2006: 26–28) PCS model can be used to explain the complex workings of oppression, how it operates and how it is reproduced. He outlines three embedded and inter-connected levels of oppression: P (the personal or psychological level), C (the cultural level), S (the structural level). The P level represents internalised, individual ideas, beliefs and atti-tudes that are held as 'truths' about the self and others and which shape responses to particular circumstances or people. The C level describes a shared consensus about 'norms' specifically, what or who is considered good, right, deviant and so on, these norms form the basis of shared values and behaviours and, often unwritten or unspoken, rules and codes of conduct. The S level, is comprised of social structures through which social divisions are perpetuated, formal-ised, legislated and institutionalised. In the model, the Personal level exists within and is influ-enced by the Cultural level which is in turn located within and determined by the Structural level.

Let us take sexual orientation as an example to further elucidate this point. We can examine the ways in which oppression, or emancipation, may be experienced by particular groups across these three interconnected levels. At the P level a young person that identifies as gay may feel different or excluded or develop feelings of low self-worth, they may experience homophobic language, bullying or violence from other individuals. These individual responses are shaped by the C level, within which heterosexuality is positioned as the default norm in society. (If you doubt this, consider the last time a 'straight' young person had to come out to their family and friends!) Cultural artefacts such as children's toys, books, media portray heteronormative narrat-ives reinforcing heterosexuality as the norm. At the S level, many recent legislative changes reflect attempts to shift these norms, however, examination of historic social policy demonstrates clear discrimination towards homosexuals: homosexual acts were not decriminalised in North-ern Ireland until 1981; Thatcher's government ratified Section 28 of the Local Government Act

1988, a legal amendment stating that a local authority 'shall not intentionally promote homosexuality or publish material with the intention of promoting homosexuality', which was designed to prevent the discussion of homosexuality particularly in schools, this was repealed in 2003; it was as late as 1994 that the legal age of consent for young gay men was reduced from 18 to 16 in line with heterosexual young people and, of course, it is only since 2013 that same sex marriage laws have been passed in England. All of these structural devices shape the ways in which sexuality is viewed and conceptualised in society, which in turn nurture cultural norms and which subsequently produce personal perceptions of sexuality.

In order to fully understand experiences of oppression and how these may be tackled, both for and among young people, it is essential that practitioners are able to offer reflection on the ways in which these become manifest not only through personal experience or prejudice, but also through cultural, social historical, political, economic and structural forces.

The youth work relationship

This chapter has already gone some way to explore the interactions between youth workers and young people that underpin good youth work, however, since relationships are the heart of youth work practice it is necessary here to attempt to specify the particular nature of these relationships. These kind of professional relationships 'should be understood as a relationship of professional friendship, as an educative and supportive friendship' (Batsleer 2008: 106). Youth work relationships differ from those with other professionals engaging young people, while youth workers are educators, they are different to teachers; while they are concerned with well-being and health, they are different to doctors and social workers; while they are friendly and concerned with association and recreation, they are different to friends. The informal nature of youth work means that the relationships produced are in turn more informal, they resemble friendships in that workers and young people engage in genuine discussion and examination of their lives, share new and challenging experiences, ask 'big questions' of one another and often enjoy just 'being with' one another. Young people, particularly those with fewer positive relationships with others, especially adults, see youth workers as trustworthy people they can confide in about aspects of their lives they may keep hidden from others. However, while youth workers are friendly, some even describe portions of their work as 'befriending young people', they are not friends. As a result it is crucial that youth work relationships exist within professional boundaries. However, these boundaries will be context dependent as suggested in the NYA (2004) statement for ethical conduct, for example, some case workers will provide young people with a mobile phone number on which they can be contacted outside of working hours, whilst others will only be in contact with young people during scheduled youth work sessions; some youth work projects will have a zero tolerance policy and sanctions for swearing within the setting, whereas other settings will prioritise this beneath a desire to develop sustained engagement with marginalised young people. Therefore, it is important for young people to be made aware of the particular expectations and boundaries within these settings and for these to be applied consistently. This is particularly important in terms of agreed levels of confidentiality, which must be outlined early on in the youth work relationship.

As a detached youth worker (not attached to a youth centre, and instead delivering youth work on the streets in areas where young people congregate), I used to include a brief explanation of confidentiality in my opening spiel when approaching new groups:

> I'm your neighbourhood youth worker, you can talk to me about anything, but there are some things I can keep confidential and some that I have to pass along. If you tell me that you have experimented with drugs, or shoplifted at the local supermarket, or think you might be pregnant, I don't have to tell anyone and we can just talk it through together. If you tell me you are being abused or are planning to kill somebody I have to pass this information on.

Such early declarations may seem strange, and are often met with laughter from the young people, but they are essential in establishing early on the parameters of the relationship and ensuring the development of safe spaces for self-expression and learning. Youth work relationships are negotiated and renegotiated between workers and young people, and strengthened by their voluntary nature as described above. It is these very relationships that many young people come to value above the resources, activities and opportunities that youth projects provide, one young person commented 'I first came to youth club because I wanted to play pool with my mates, I keep coming because of the youth workers, they really care about me and they help me.' Many poorly subsidised and subsequently, poorly furnished youth clubs remain popular because of such valued relationships.

Many consider relationships to be the cornerstone of youth work, but how are we to evaluate this within neoliberal systems of monitoring? The very foundation of the work is the quality of the relationship between worker and young person and yet they are virtually impossible to quantify:

> How can workers score and gauge the effect we may be having on others, let alone calculate the value that someone else chooses to place on their relationship with us? ... Even if we do not consciously 'educate' or 'counsel' but spend our time 'being' with someone, then we may be doing something of incalculable value.
>
> (Blacker 2010: 30)

ACTIVITY 3

Consider relationships you have had with adults in your life, both positive and negative. How did these relationships differ? How did you become aware of the norms and boundaries of these relationships? How did you decide which adults you could trust?

Remembering the 'community' in youth and community work

Thus far this chapter has focussed specifically on 'youth work', however, it is important to note that youth and community workers operate in diverse settings and youth and community studies degrees prepare students for work with community groups more broadly. The principles explored above, voluntarism, universality, association, anti-oppressive practice and informal education, are also shared and shaped by 'community work'. In one sense, we can conceptualise youth work as being encompassed within the broader field of community work, in that youth projects often reflect wider community agendas, and in many cases youth workers seek to make links between groups of young people and the wider community. However, there will also be opportunities for students to experience community settings that are targeted at adults. Communities may be either geographical in nature or arise from a shared interest, and we can consider community work to be 'the process of assisting people to improve their own communities by undertaking autonomous collective action' (Twelvetrees 2008: 1). Steeped in a long tradition of citizen participation, empowerment and public voice, community work is concerned, like youth work, with tackling oppression and inequality and drawing solutions to locally identified issues with local actors.

Youth and community placement case studies

Case study 1: the youth club

Steven was a 20-year-old undergraduate. During the first year of his degree, Steven undertook a placement in an open-access youth centre in West London. He attended on Monday evenings from 5.30pm until 9.30pm. The young people attending the centre were 13 to 19 years old, and they were a mixed gender and mixed ethnicity group. The setting was a local authority run youth club that provided a variety of activities at each session including sports, craft activities and issued-based activities focussing on topics raised by the young people such as drugs, sexual health, mental health and so on. This is Steven's reflection on placement:

> I was very nervous to begin my first placement, the youth centre was in quite a rough area and I was worried that the young people I would be working with would be challenging or even scary. At my first session I was also worried that, being so young, and so close in age to the young people, would mean that they wouldn't take me seriously. I spoke to the youth worker-in-charge and she helped to put me at ease. She told me that the young people would take their cue from me, if I displayed a professional manner, acted as a role model and emulated the behaviour of the other youth workers, the young people would treat me like a youth worker. She was right. That is not to say that they didn't test me out! At one session I was really pleased because two of the girls had some really meaningful conversations with me, they told me lots of things about

their lives that they wouldn't have told many other people, if I'm honest I was shocked by some of the things they told me – stories of drugs and parties and getting into trouble. Their teenage years were worlds apart from my own. By the end of session I really felt that I was being trusted and accepted. As they were leaving they told me that they had stolen chocolate bars from the tuck shop. They said, 'it's okay to tell you because you're one of us, you won't grass to the other youth workers'. I wasn't sure what to do, I didn't want to ruin the rapport we had built up and I was worried that if I told the other youth workers what they had done they would never trust me again. In the end I reported it to the rest of the staff and the girls were tackled about it at the next session. It was a difficult thing to do but I realised that as a student on placement it was my job to uphold the rules of the setting and that I had a duty to be honest with the rest of the team. This was just the first of a number of ethical dilemmas that I experienced on placement, and I came to realise that being a professional youth worker is all about making decisions like this, about balancing relationships with young people, with what is best for them. The most important lessons that I took away from my placement came from those ethical dilemmas.

Case study 2: the homeless project

Melissa, 18 and Rachel, 18 undertook a placement during their second year of undergraduate study. They were placed together at a drop-in project in the South West. They attended the drop-in sessions on Thursday afternoons. The client group of the project were people aged 16 upwards who were either homeless or financially disadvantaged, they attended the project to access the food and clothes bank, to take a shower, eat a hot meal, gain advice from staff and to socialise. These are their reflections on placement:

MELISSA: I don't think it's possible to put into words how much of impact going to the homeless project has had on me. I was absolutely shocked to find out how difficult some people's lives are, and I was actually pretty shaken after my first visit. At the very first drop-in one of the members of staff had to shave a woman's head! She had been homeless for some time and her hair was in such a bad state that she just asked the staff to shave it all off. It sounds like a silly thing to be shaken by, but it just seemed so extreme to me. The woman even said, 'it's better to not be too pretty when you're living on the street', that really hit me hard. I always knew that some people were homeless but I don't think I wanted to think about what that is really like. Since going on placement to the homeless project I've changed my outlook on a lot of things. I carried on volunteering at the project after my placement finished. I've chosen modules that have a more sociological and political focus. I have arranged two fundraising events to try to give back to the homeless project. I'm doing an education studies degree and I no longer only see teaching as the career path afterwards. I want to do something to work with people in those kinds of circumstances.

RACHEL: Doing my placement at the homeless project was definitely an eye-opener! When I was allocated the placement I had an idea in my mind of the kinds of people that I might meet, and I really got it wrong. I thought that the people using the project would be alcoholics or drug addicts or seriously disturbed or something, I can't believe I'm even saying that now. The people I met were nothing like those stereotypes, they were normal people, some of them had degrees themselves. They just found themselves in a bad situation and couldn't get out of it. A big learning curve for me was realising that I had to prove myself to the people coming to the project. I was so concerned with not seeming judgemental towards them that I overlooked the fact that they might find me under-qualified to work with them! I learned that I had to work hard to build trust, and I had to accept that I didn't necessarily have the power or resources to help them. It was a life changing experience going to the homeless project and I'm so glad I had the opportunity to go there on placement.

These case studies demonstrate the possibilities that exist through youth and community work placements for transformative learning. The students in the previous examples gained, not only workplace skills, professional values and practice based knowledge from engaging with practice, but also developed radically new perspectives on their conceptualisations of the social world. Spending time in these setting offered opportunities to revise previously held assumptions, challenge stereotypes and reflect on their own role in organisations designed to work with marginalised groups.

ACTIVITY 4

Use the Internet to identify a local youth and community project. Try to discover the purpose or 'mission statement' of the organisation, the client group that it is aimed at, and the activities of the project. Consider what assumptions you might have about this project and the people that might attend.

Top tips for a successful youth and community work placement

This chapter has sought to give students a very brief introduction to the overarching values and methods of youth and community work, to set out what to expect from experiences in these kinds of placements. I would like to conclude by drawing on these to provide my top tips for a successful youth and community work placement:

1   Remember you are there to learn, take in as much information as you can, observe workers in practice, ask questions, try things out for yourself and don't be afraid to make mistakes. Supervising youth workers do not expect you to know everything

before you arrive and will value a willingness to learn and reflect. This process of reflecting and learning does not set you apart from the qualified youth workers, rather it aligns you with their own practice. Observe youth workers in action, try to find opportunities to see how all staff in the setting operate so you can compare and learn different styles of working. Try to experience all elements of the setting rather remaining in one area. Youth workers by their very nature are usually keen to share their knowledge with others.

2   Be a professional. While youth and community settings are far more informal in nature than many other education settings, with more flexible working practices and more informal approaches to relationships building, you are still there as a role model to the young people. If you are unsure about exactly how to display a professional youth work attitude, take your cue from your placement supervisor. Establish before you arrive the correct dress code. Be reliable and punctual, it is likely that if you are undertaking a placement within a small organisation, they will quickly become reliant upon you – settings that must adhere to client/staff ratios may, in the event of staff sickness, rely upon your presence to be able to open their doors. Familiarise yourself with the particular policies and procedures of your setting, ensure that you know who you should speak to about particular aspects of your role such as safeguarding, health and safety or other concerns.

3   Be cautious in building relationships with young people. There is a fine line to negotiate between being friendly and being a friend. Often students fall into the trap of becoming friends with young people. As a new member of staff the young people will test your boundaries. They will want to discover whether they can persuade you to deviate from the norms of the setting. Ensure that you establish with your supervisor how behaviour is managed in your setting and always share concerns, disclosures by young people and rule breaks with your supervisor – youth work is a team endeavour and this is one of its strengths. Understand that the young people may choose to develop working relationships with you very quickly and may even come to rely upon you – never make promises that you cannot keep. While it may be flattering to find that a young person trusts you and wishes to confide in you, be mindful to avoid creating dependence. Remember that you will be attending the placement for a limited period of time and therefore creating such dependence is likely to cause feelings of abandonment in the young person when you withdraw. Always share important information that a young person shares with you with your supervising youth worker, this is not a breach of confidentiality since team working is the norm in youth work, and young people understand that information is shared between workers.

4   Never say no to an opportunity to get involved, if a youth worker relinquishes control of an activity or session to you, it is a demonstration of trust. It is understandable that sessions may not go to plan, or that you may feel things should have been done better

or differently, these are rich opportunities for reflection and learning. Involvement in some activities may push outside your comfort zone, not everyone is keen to engage in street dance sessions with young people or discuss sexually transmitted diseases! Challenge yourself to be involved as far as possible, these shared experiences help to build trusting, reciprocal relationships with young people, not to mention providing opportunities for personal growth. When you become settled into a setting you might be asked to plan an activity. This may seem a daunting prospect, however, there are many sources of inspiration to draw from on the Internet, from other youth workers and from the young people themselves. Always brief your supervisor before carrying activities out so that they can check for suitability.

5   Be grateful and humble, remember that in times of austerity, where youth services are underfunded and understaffed, providing and supervising placements can add to the already significant workload of youth work practitioners. Thank the supervisor for having you at their setting! It is also important to remember that the settings encompass a wide variety of skill sets and roles, session leaders may not hold professional qualifications, or sessions may be organised and led predominantly by young people, remember that they are still the experts at the setting. On occasion you may not immediately understand why particular rules or procedures have been devised, keep in mind that the youth workers have more experience and insider knowledge on young people and the overall setting than you. Do not be overly critical of the setting or people in it. Instead ask questions to clarify.

6   Enjoy yourself! There are few work placements that include such vibrant settings with such an exciting variety of activities: sports, arts, politics, conversation and so on, and there is the potential for every visit to your placement to be a unique learning experience. While youth work can sometimes be frustrating, it is also extremely rewarding and being allowed access to young people's worlds is a privilege that cannot be overstated.

References

Batsleer, J. (2008) *Informal Learning in Youth Work*. London: Sage.

Blacker, H. (2010) 'Relationships, Friendship and Youth Work'. In Jeffs, T. and Smith, M.K. eds *Youth Work Practice*. Basingstoke: Palgrave Macmillan: 15–30.

Board of Education (1939) *The Service of Youth, Circular 1486*. London: HMSO.

Bright, G. ed. (2015) *Youth Work: Histories, Policies and Contexts*. London: Palgrave Macmillan.

Bradford, S. (2012) *Sociology, Youth and Youth Work Practice*. Basingstoke: Palgrave Macmillan.

Bradford, S. (2015) 'State Beneficence or Government Control'. In Bright, G. ed. *Youth Work: Histories, Policies and Contexts*. London: Palgrave Macmillan: 22–35.

Chouhan, J. (2009) 'Anti-Oppressive Practice'. In Wood, J. and Hine, J. eds *Work with Young People*. London: Sage: 60–75.

Dominelli, L. (2002) *Anti Oppressive Social Work Theory and Practice*. Basingstoke: Palgrave Macmillan.

Ingram, G. and Harris, J. (2013) 'Defining Good Youth Work'. In Curran, S., Harrison, R. and Mackinnon, D. eds *Working with Young People*. London: Sage: 69–72.

Jeffs, T. and Smith, M.K. (1996) *Informal Education: Conversation, Democracy and Learning*. London: Educational Heretics Press.

Jeffs, T. and Smith, M.K. eds (2010) *Youth Work Practice*. Basingstoke: Palgrave Macmillan.

Lifelong Learning UK (2008) *National Occupational Standards for Youth Work*. London: LLUK.

Ministry of Education (1960) *The Youth Service in England and Wales*. London: HMSO.

National Youth Agency, (2004) *Ethical Conduct in Youth Work: a Statement of Values and Principles*. Leicester: NYA.

Payne, M. (2009) 'Modern Youth Work: "Purity" or Common Cause'. In Wood, J.J. and Hine, J. eds *Work with Young People: Theory and Policy for Practice*. London: Sage: 213–232.

Sercombe, H. (2015) 'In the Service of the State: Youth Work Under New Labour'. In Bright, G. ed. *Youth Work: Histories, Policies and Contexts*. London: Palgrave Macmillan: 38–57.

Smith, M. 2008 'Informal Learning', the Encyclopaedia of Informal Education [online]. Available from: www.infed.org/biblio/inf-lrn.htm.

Thompson, N. (2006) *Anti-Discriminatory Practice*. 4th edn, Basingstoke: Palgrave.

Twelvetrees, A. (2008) *Community Work*. 4th edn. Basingstoke: Palgrave Macmillan.

Tyler, M. (2009) *Managing Modern Youth Work: Empowering Youth and Community Work Practice*. Exeter: Learning Matters.

Wood, J., Westwood, S. and Thompson, G. (2015) *Youth Work: Preparation for Practice*. London: Routledge.

Young, K. (1999) *The Art of Youth Work*. London: Russell House.

12

Work-based learning in the early years

How everyday experiences in early years settings can provide a secure foundation for academic study

Martine Duggan

Purpose of the chapter

After reading this chapter you should understand:

- the nature of critical reflection;

- how the experiences gained in the early years can provide a solid foundation for academic study.

Work-based learning in the early years – a brief overview

Since the mid 1990s there has been unprecedented interest in the early years sector (Hammond *et al.* 2015), with significant government investment directed towards the goal of 'the professionalism and the upskilling' of the early years workforce (HM Government 2007). Work-based programmes, which are generally designed through the collaboration of employers, universities and further education colleges, provide both an academic and work-based component (Burke *et al.* 2009), enabling students on placement or those employed within a setting, to 'learn while doing' (Rowley 2005). Seen as a means to help combat poverty, improve opportunities for children and engage parents back into the workforce (Farrelly 2010), a high quality early years workforce was a priority on the New Labour government's 'transformational reform' agenda (Miller 2008). To this end, in 2001, the 'Senior Practitioner' status was introduced for those working with children from birth to eight years. This status was attained through successful completion of the Early Years Sector-Endorsed Foundation Degree (EYSEFD); a vocational qualification, designed to integrate academic study with work-based learning (Miller 2008). The Foundation Degree is just one of the many formal qualifications or awards, for which early years work-based learners can gain accreditation. Others include: the full BA (hons); Early Years Teacher Status (EYTS); Early Years Educator (EYE), as well as post graduate qualifications such as the Post Graduate Certificate in Education, (PGCE) and Masters. This chapter aims to support and encourage those work-based learners who are seeking to gain such formal accreditation, however, it is important to appreciate the multiple other personal and professional reasons why practitioners might engage in informal study, research or work-based investigations. As Callan and Reed (2011) suggest, practitioners may want to improve practice, to inform parents, to find out more in order to lead or change practice, because an inspection is imminent or to aid professional development. Although the outcome of such endeavours might not lead to a formal qualification, early years settings can be described as natural research sites, in which practitioners are already using the critically reflective 'skills, the attitude and the ability to engage in enquiry' (Callan and Reed 2011: 8). And at the heart of such practice lies critically reflective practice, as shall now be explained.

'Critically reflective practice'

Consider

- What does the term 'critically' reflective practice mean to you?
- How does 'critically reflective' practice differ from reflective practice?
- Think of a recent example where you were critically reflective – what was the context and the outcome?

The centrality of reflective practice in the early years sector is widely acknowledged (Canning and Reed 2010; Craft and Paige-Smith 2008; Farrelly 2010; Rose and Rogers 2012). The Early Years Foundation Stage (EYFS) Statutory Framework makes explicit reference to this pedagogical tool, as it states: practitioners should reflect on the different ways that children learn (DfE 2014).

Indirect reference is also made through the specific requirements that are arguably underpinned by the reflective process; for example, the Statutory Guidance states there should: be a 'culture of self-improvement'; with opportunities made to 'identify solutions to address issues as they arise'.

Historically, within experiential learning discourses, the ubiquitous term 'reflective practice' has been open to multiple and varied interpretations. Mezirow (1991) suggests reflection is generally used as a synonym for 'higher-order mental' processes. Akin to this perspective,

Boud *et al.* (1985) describe reflection as a generic term for intellectual and affective activities, which lead to new understandings and appreciation. Whereas Jordi (2011) highlights the reputation that reflection holds for distilling 'rational knowledge' from the mess of human experience. Stephen Brookfield (1995) adds a further helpful dimension with his perspective on the notion of a 'critically' reflective thinker. According to Brookfield, as individuals, we will be in a better position to make informed and rational decisions on our practice if we have looked at it from as many different vantage points as possible. To this end, he advocates a model to support critical reflection, which comprises four 'lenses'. When we reflect critically on our practice we should aim to look through all of these lenses; that is, through the lens of our own autobiographies, from the eyes of the children, from the perspective of our colleagues and that of the theoretical literature.

Rose and Rogers (2012) adopt a more nuanced position with respect to the particular context of the early years. They draw the distinction between 'reflective thinking' and 'critical reflection'. Reflective thinking, they explain, is the ability to think back on an experience in an evaluative way in order to improve the quality of provision. Although similar, the concept of critical reflection has a broader application; for the critically reflective practitioner not only strives to meet the child's interests and needs, but also to ensure the provision is inclusive and anti-discriminatory. This ethical perspective aligns with that of educational thinkers such as Freire (1996) and Dahlberg and Moss (2005), who espouse critical pedagogy. Adding 'critical' to pedagogy represents a commitment to generate social justice, and freedom from oppressive educational practices. As MacNaughton (2005: 9) explains, a critical pedagogue will 'examine the social and political factors that produce dominant educational knowledge and practices, and to ask whose interests they serve'. A critical pedagogue will thus be sensitised to the inequalities that can be perpetuated by educational organisations. These critical themes and the capacity practitioners have to engage with them will be explored in more detail later, but now attention will turn to the related and fundamental practice of problem solving.

Problem solving lies at the heart of early years practice; as noted earlier, the EYFS requires practitioners to identify solutions in order to address issues as they arise. On a daily basis, and throughout each day, it is fair to say early years practitioners will likely face a range of dilemmas, predicaments or issues relating to children and their families; and these necessitate an informed, rational decision to achieve a positive outcome. Many of these problems will be dealt with in a matter of seconds, whilst others warrant a deeper level of reflection before any transformative action is taken. Take for example, a practitioner, who seeks to extend a child's learning. The executive decision to support the child will typically be based on a range of interrelated factors such as: the child's socio-cultural, psychological, physical and emotional needs, their interests, intentions, wishes and pedagogical history. Such decisions will, of course, be context specific but may well involve the practitioner exercising some of the following cognitive functions: she might reflect on when, how or whether to intervene; she may evaluate the effect or influence her presence may be having on the child; she may question the validity or accuracy of the expectations or assumptions she might harbour towards the child; she may evaluate the quality of the environment and how it needs to be adapted; she may analyse whether the child would benefit from more open-ended resources, whether the child's intentions are being accurately interpreted or whether there are any avoidable obstacles which are preventing or impeding the child from learning. She may collaborate by listening to and discussing other ideas, such as those from colleagues or the child's family. These executive functions, carried out throughout the day, will continue beyond the micro adult: child interaction, and will extend, for example, into the broader context of improving provision.

The following account documents how a practitioner approaches and solves one particular problem that presented in her setting.

Task

Read the following account and reflect on how she approaches the problem:

■ From which vantage points does she look at the problem?

■ How does her approach compare to the way you addressed a recent problem?

■ How did you go about it?

■ What different lenses did you look though, before acting?

The practitioner explains:

> We recently looked at how we could improve provision on the top floor. In order for me to do that, I looked at the rooms we had and how we were currently using them but to actually really improve it and offer something completely different to what we are offering now, I had to really look at what other people were doing; what people had written about the subject, as well as doing mini action research, auditing areas and talking to the children about what they were interested in. So looking at what works well, what doesn't work so well and what are other people saying, and how other people are doing it, it's actually bringing that together to produce something different to move forward.
>
> (Early Years Teacher, Private Nursery)

A deconstruction and analysis of this practitioner's account reveals a number of perceived parallels or overlaps with the 'higher-order' critical thinking dispositions and abilities required in the sphere of scholarly activity. Critical thinking is considered central to higher levels of education, and a fundamental goal of learning (Kuhn 1999). Significantly, any scholarly research activity will involve critical thinking (Moon 2008). According to Ennis (1987) the associated dispositions and abilities integral to critical thinking fall into two closely related categories; the ability to reflect sceptically and the ability to think in a reasoned way. These dual abilities appear embedded in the above approach taken by the practitioner, as shall now be explained.

Reflecting sceptically

In terms of 'reflecting sceptically', the practitioner presents as an open-minded individual, who does not make a decision based on limited evidence. The choices she makes in transforming the room are not based on just one source of evidence, but rather are built on evidence gathered through multiple lenses. In a sense she remains sceptical and is suspending judgement until she has developed as full a picture as possible, thus, she is 'holding open the possibility that what you know at any given time may be only part of the picture' (Cottrell 2005: 3). By the same token, and in terms of similar processes, remaining sceptical is considered to be a valuable attribute or discipline that lies at the heart of scholarly activity. Rather than accepting at surface level what an author or theorist might claim, without questioning its legitimacy, a critical thinker will actively engage with and interrogate the validity of the claims made. In order to critically analyse and evaluate the accuracy, the critical thinker will cross-reference to other sources of evidence, such as one's own practice, or other literature. By doing this she will be in a better position to mount a challenge to established theory. In the same vein, a critical researcher, who is presenting their own claims or argument in an assignment or work-based report, will know that to convince a 'sceptical readership' i.e. the marker, they will need to present a critical stance, which is not one dimensional, but substantiated by the weight of literature and other forms of evidence, such as their own practice.

Thinking in a reasoned way

Through the above account we can see that the practitioner is also demonstrating her capacity to reason or use rational thought to improve practice and outcomes for children. Reasoning involves 'analysing evidence and drawing conclusions from it' (Cottrell 2005: 3). In this context, the practitioner identifies, selects and synthesises the information she has gathered in order to draw a precise and an informed conclusion on how to proceed. Her reasoning process relies on the capacity to organise, make sense of and evaluate the data she is gathering. Unless she can do this, the judgements (i.e. which inform the plans she implements for the room) will not necessarily be rational, logical or well informed. Again this approach resonates with key cognitive processes involved in academic study. These will involve both critically analysing other people's reasoning as well as knowing and presenting one's own reasons. In order to engage with or construct an argument, the reader or writer needs to be clear on the reasoning that underpins the argument. Without this key ingredient it is difficult to accept the logic of any conclusions drawn.

Critical thinking goes hand in hand with the capacity to construct an argument. When constructing an argument, a particular challenge for some students is to decide on which line of enquiry, or which 'thread' should be developed from the mass of information that is available, as the following work-based learner explains:

> Building an argument was tricky, it can be difficult, you almost don't know which bits are relevant and which bits aren't to help you build your thread.

A practitioner, who had recently completed her BA (hons) in Early Years offers helpful insights into the nature of the analytical skills developed though her practice, which have an application for academic writing. She acknowledges the confidence she needed to be able to identify and select a single aspect to focus on, rather than trying to cover too broad an area in insufficient detail:

> I think it's partly about not being frightened and having the confidence to look at one thing in detail, for instance, I was looking recently, observing children playing with one of our play pods and I was talking to some other colleagues about documenting – they were finding it difficult to document because there was so much and they said we just can't write it all down but I said it's actually about being able to focus on just one child within the group, that one child – to see for example, how are they interacting with the other children, but to actually be prepared to focus on just one thing, you can look at it in real detail then, rather than trying to get the big picture and only get to the surface of it. My mentor has always encouraged me to go deeper and more narrow, rather than going wider.

Early years educator

This account reveals how the practitioner has developed her attentional processes to good effect. With a discerning and astute attitude, rather than trying to cover too much, she demonstrates the capacity to home in and distinguish what she perceives to be a salient aspect on which to focus; and importantly, this becomes her frame of reference for further action. The same judicious principles apply when engaging in scholarly activity. When seeking to detect and understand a complex or challenging argument presented by an author, a student might well need to decode the author's position in order to fully grasp and engage with their line of reasoning. To this end the student will need to home in and quickly get to the heart of the matter (that is the gist of the argument) by attending to the most relevant material. Similarly, when mounting one's own argument, in order to be persuasive, the student will need to identify and select or prioritise a line of reasoning or a thread on which to base her argument.

A practitioner, who had achieved EYPS through work-based learning placements, highlights the perceived parallels between her everyday reflective practice and writing for academic purposes. In both situations it is noted that the critical skill of evaluation is deployed. She explains:

> Within a setting, you generally tend to think about something you're doing and the things that affect the thing that you are doing, you know … what went well and what didn't go so well, you then start thinking about and evaluating how you can overcome, change and adapt things. Now that process fits well with the academic writing, because when you write an essay, you start with a question or a problem you want to analyse, and you look at what you already believe and then you bring in other ideas, you evaluate them and that's very much the same as your everyday reflective practice, so there are definite parallels in that respect.

Imaginative speculation

According to Brookfield (1995), one of the key activities central to critical reflection is that of 'imaginative speculation'. This process is where thinkers rely on their imagination to think of alternative, better ways of doing things; in other words 'thinking outside the box'. The following account provides further insights into how the everyday creative practices within the early years overlap with the creative demands of academic writing:

> With children when you're doing problem solving and you're extending their learning, writing an essay is based on a similar format, so with the children you're thinking about how can I extend that child's learning? … by perhaps going off in a completely different direction to what they thought about but actually when you write an essay you can do the same; thinking this is what so and so thinks but what about this? What if I go in a completely different direction and I thought about it from this perspective? Has anyone else thought about it from this angle? What ideas do they have and how do they link to the original idea I had? I think because with children you're always thinking of creative ways to solve problems, and it's the same with writing an essay.
>
> (Early Years Practitioner and Masters Student)

Consider

Think of recent examples of where you have approached a practical situation in a creative way:

- In what way was it creative?
- How does this relate to your approach taken when engaging in study? Can you identify any similarities in the approach taken?

Working towards social justice

Another key potential of the early years practitioner's role is to actively engage with and contribute to the social justice agenda. A practical example of how this prospect manifests lies in the government funded two-year-old early education entitlement. This intervention programme enables eligible two year olds to receive free early education and care places, and is crucially targeted at those families who meet the eligibility criteria, such as those on income support, universal credit, or those receiving support through part 6 of the Immigration and Asylum Act. Thus practitioners who support these children and their families are addressing social justice by helping to reduce the gap between 'advantaged' and 'disadvantaged' children. As the purpose of the programme is to improve the latter's social and cognitive outcomes, for example, their social confidence and independence, and their verbal skills and reasoning ability (Smith *et al.* 2009).

Interestingly, through my experience as a university lecturer supporting students to achieve level 6 and 7 qualifications, I have found early years work-based learners respond particularly well to the literature and themes around the social justice agenda. For example, these learners are generally adept at engaging confidently and enthusiastically with challenging constructs and themes relating to marginalisation processes, dominant ideologies, power structures and dynamics, oppressive practices such as stereotyping and the harbouring of negative assumptions towards certain groups. I have noticed how these students very quickly get to grips with and become passionately absorbed with some of the more complex literature on critical pedagogy. This interest, coupled with a genuine ethical stance, stands them in good stead when completing assignments with a social justice underpinning; in other words where the focus is on improving outcomes for all groups. A practitioner provides suggestions as to why she relates so well to the social justice agenda; revealing how her practical experience of working ethically with children and families gives her a perceived advantage over those students, who may not be work-based:

> Working in most settings you will have already have a working understanding of social justice … you will have particular children and families in mind when you start talking about these issues, your experiences are already there and you can understand the effects of it, you know you can see it and know how it works and understand it already. Whereas maybe people who are learning about it who perhaps haven't worked in the sector, they won't have had first hand understanding of what that actually means necessarily. You can really relate to it … it really matters. So when we talked about it on the course, in my mind I already had families and children that popped into my head – it already meant something to me, because I already felt the importance of it on behalf of these people I work with.
>
> (Practitioner, Early Years Setting)

Conclusion

This chapter has explored how the nature of early years practice can provide a valuable foundation for the scholarly challenges of academic study. Early years practitioners fulfil a complex role as they are charged with the significant responsibility of improving outcomes for children and their families. As has been suggested, to be effective in this field requires an astute, creative and enquiring mind and the deployment of a wide range of critical skills. Yet in spite of the laudable and challenging nature of their work, the status and pay of the early years practitioner remains relatively low (Vincent and Brown 2010). Gaining formal accreditation for work-based learning can raise one's confidence, boost morale and have a significant impact on children's outcomes. Importantly it can also help to raise the status of the early years workforce. Work-based learners are experts with a first-hand knowledge and understanding of their field. It is this practical expertise, which enhances, enriches and makes academic study meaningful. And it is this expertise that needs greater acknowledgement.

Further reading

Callan, S. and Reed, M. (2011) *Work-based Research in the Early Years*. London: Sage.

Farrelly, P. (2010) *Early Years Work-Based Learning*. Exeter: Learning Matters Ltd.

MacNaughton, G. (2005) *Doing Foucault in Early Childhood Studies Applying Poststructural Ideas*. Abingdon: Routledge.

References

Boud, D., Keogh, R. and Walker, D. (1985) *Reflection: Turning Experience into Learning*. London: Kogan Page.

Brookfield, S. (1995) *Becoming a Critically Reflective Teacher*. San Franciso, CA: Jossey-Bass.

Burke, L., Marks-Maran, D.J., Ooms, A., Webb, M. and Cooper, D. (2009) 'Towards a Pedagogy of Work-Based Learning: Perceptions of Work-Based Learning in Foundation Degrees'. *Journal of Vocational Education and Training* 61 (1): 15–33.

Callan, S. and Reed, M. (2011) *Work-Based Research in the Early Years*. London: Sage.

Cottrell, S. (2005) *Critical Thinking Skills: Developing Effective Analysis and Argument*. Basingstoke: Palgrave Macmillan.

Craft, A. and Paige Smith, A. (2008) *Developing Reflective Practice in the Early Years*. Maidenhead: Open University Press.

Dahlberg, G. and Moss, P. (2005) *Ethics and Politics in Early Childhood Education*. London: Routledge-Falmer.

Department for Education (DfE) (2014) *Statutory Framework for the Early Years Foundation Stage*.

Ennis, R.H. (1987) 'A Taxonomy of Critical Thinking Dispositions and Abilities' in Baron. J. and Sternberg, R. eds *Teaching Thinking Skills: Theory and Practice*. New York: W.H. Freeman: 9–26.

Farrelly, P. (2010) *Early Years Work-Based Learning*. Exeter: Learning Matters Ltd.

Freire, P. (1996) *Pedagogy of the Oppressed*. London: Penguin.

Hammond, S., Powell, S. and Smith, K. (2015) 'Towards Mentoring as Feminist Praxis in Early Childhood Education and Care in England'. *Early Years: An International Research Journal* 35 (2): 139–153.

HM Government (2007) *Children's Workforce Strategy Update Spring 2007*. London: HMSO.

Jordi, R. (2011) 'Reframing the Concept of Reflection: Consciousness, Experiential Learning, and Reflective Learning Practices'. *Adult Education Quarterly* 61 (2): 181–197.

Kuhn, D. (1999) 'A Developmental Model of Critical Thinking'. *Educational Researcher* 28 (2): 16–26.

MacNaughton, G. (2005) *Doing Foucault in Early Childhood Studies Applying Poststructural Ideas*. Abingdon: Routledge.

Mezirow, J. (1991) *Transformational Dimensions of Adult Learning*. San Francisco, CA: Jossey Bass.

Miller, L. (2008) 'Developing Professionalism within a Regulatory Framework in England: Challenges and Possibilities'. *European Early Childhood Education Research Journal* 16 (2): 255–268.

Moon, J. (2008) *Critical Thinking: An Exploration of Theory and Practice*. Abingdon: Routledge.

Reed, M. and Canning, N. (2010) *Reflective Practice in the Early Years*. London: Sage.

Rose, J. and Rogers, S. (2012) *The Role of the Adult in Early Years Settings*. Maidenhead: Open University Press.

Rowley, J. (2005) 'Foundation Degrees: a Risky Business?' *Quality Assurance in Education* 13 (1): 6–16.

Smith, R., Purdon, S., Schneider, V., La Valle, I., Wollny, I., Owen, R. and Bryson, C. (2009) *Early Education Pilot for Two Year Old Children Evaluation*. London: National Centre for Social Research.

Vincent, C. and Braun, A. (2010) 'And Hairdressers Are Quite Seedy …: The Moral Worth of Childcare Training'. *Contemporary Issues in Early Childhood Education* 11 (2): 203–214.

Vincent, C. and Braun, A. (2011) '"I think a Lot of It Is Common Sense. …" Early Years Students, Professionalism and the Development of a "Vocational Habitus"'. *Journal of Education Policy* 26 (6): 771–785.

Index